Libraries Designed for Learning

by Scott Bennett
November 2003

Council on Library and Information Resources

Washington, D.C.

About the Author

Scott Bennett is Yale University Librarian Emeritus. He has had extensive experience with library planning, construction, renovation, and restoration at Yale and in his service as the Sheridan director of the Milton S. Eisenhower Library, Johns Hopkins University, and as assistant university librarian for collection management at Northwestern University. He has also served on both the library and the English department faculties of the University of Illinois at Urbana-Champaign.

ISBN 1-932326-05-7

Published by:

Council on Library and Information Resources
1755 Massachusetts Avenue, NW, Suite 500
Washington, DC 20036
Web site at http://www.clir.org

Additional copies are available for $20 per copy. Orders must be placed through CLIR's Web site.

 The paper in this publication meets the minimum requirements of the American National Standard for Information Sciences—Permanence of Paper for Printed Library Materials ANSI Z39.48-1984.

Contents

Acknowledgments

The Council on Library and Information Resources (CLIR) and the Council of Independent Colleges (CIC) sponsored this report. The author is especially grateful to Deanna Marcum for her long-sustained interest in this study. The author is, however, solely responsible for the study data and their interpretation. Nothing in this report necessarily reflects the views of CLIR or CIC.

The author wishes to thank most warmly the nearly 250 academic library directors who responded to the survey that was one basis for this report. He is also deeply indebted to the 31 librarians and academic officers who agreed to be interviewed at some length for this study. The author assured all of these persons they would not be identified as individuals in the study, so they cannot be thanked here by name. But whatever merit the study may have comes directly from their generous participation.

At CLIR, Kathlin Smith provided thoughtful advice to the author at every turn, was tolerant of delays, and ably guided the study through to publication.

For other expert assistance, generously given, the author thanks Nicholas Burckel, Robert Burger, Pamela Delphenich, David DeMello, Richard Ekman, Amy Harbur, Lisa Janicke Hinchliffe, Danuta Nitecki, Susan Perry, and Nancy Roderer. The staff and the collections at the University of Illinois Library at Urbana-Champaign made it a joy to do this study. Finally, the author wishes to thank his many colleagues at Yale University—librarians, faculty, academic officers, facilities planners and managers, architects, and engineers—from whom he leaned so much about library space planning.

Preface

For centuries, people have visited libraries to find information, and the practical needs of housing collections and accommodating readers have typically driven library design. In many cases, design has reached further, to create a place that inspires the individual and the intellect. Whatever the form, library buildings have become physical symbols for the life of the mind.

As technological advances of the past 20 years have made it possible for people to find information without entering a library building, some have asked whether the bricks-and-mortar library is doomed to extinction. Yet others maintain that the growth of technology has made the library even more important because it enables access to electronic content, services, and training that would otherwise be unavailable to information seekers.

Library design and construction of the past decade have responded to changes in information technology in a variety of ways, from incorporating electronic classrooms for teaching information literacy to physically integrating the space where electronic and print materials are kept. Some libraries have created "information commons," equipped with technology and staffed by information specialists. Such developments, while responding to new technologies, have nonetheless continued to support the traditional goal of enabling the manipulation and mastery of information.

In his provocative essay, Scott Bennett asks whether the goal of libraries today might more appropriately be described as "supporting collaborative learning by which students turn information into knowledge and sometimes into wisdom." He bases his question on changes in teaching and study habits of the past 20 years—changes distinguished by an increasing emphasis on group and collaborative work. He also references recent literature on learning that discusses knowledge creation as a community project. As Joan Bechtel, whose work is noted in part 4 of this report, writes, "the new paradigm for librarianship . . . is conversation."

To what extent have recent library design projects been driven by an understanding of how students learn and how faculty teach? To find out what motivated academic library renovation and construction in the past decade and how library planning was conducted, Mr. Bennett conducted an extensive survey and did follow-up interviews with library directors and chief academic officers. He concludes that while most recent library projects serve users well, they have rarely been informed by a systematic assessment of how students learn and faculty teach. The author suggests that planning based on such an assessment could equip the library to serve an even more vital function as a space for teaching and learning.

The topic of this report is central to CLIR's interest in exploring the changing role of the library in the digital world. We are grateful to the author for bringing new insight to this question. We are also grateful to the Council on Independent Colleges, and to Richard Ekman, for supporting Mr. Bennett's early work on this topic.

Kathlin Smith
Director of Communications

INTRODUCTION

This report seeks two groups of readers: academic librarians who have significant responsibility for library construction and renovation projects, and campus academic officers who wish to engage substantively with the question of how library space can advance the core learning and teaching missions of their institutions.

Readers of this report will likely have already consulted the exceptionally useful book, *Planning Academic and Research Library Buildings*, by Philip D. Leighton and David C. Weber. For all its merits, this book simply assumes that "those undertaking a major remodeling project, an addition, or a new separate facility have some understanding of the process of analyzing an institution's mission and objectives, [and] can determine the nature of space that should be provided" (p. xxvi). The weight of this assumption is evident in the fact that this 900-page book gives only one page of text to describing academic objectives and the library (chapter 1, section 2), and just two pages to defining the building problem (chapter 1, section 4), where problems are defined primarily in terms of ordinary library operational needs. A slightly longer section, entitled Character and Nature of the Academic or Research Institution (chapter 3, section 1), is little more than an elaborated checklist of routine but important considerations in planning.

The authors of *Planning Academic and Research Library Buildings* might reasonably give little attention to such fundamental issues. It is, after all, commonly the case that severe problems with library space go unaddressed for years, or even decades, ensuring that most members of the academic community have vivid, firsthand experience of them. Living so long with problems usually leaves people certain what the problems are, eager to have them addressed, and confident in judging whether a library project has succeeded.

Where such long-accumulating problems urgently demand attention, opportunities to engage with emerging trends in student learning and faculty teaching may be less obvious and less compelling to those who set priorities and pay for buildings. This report attempts to understand how library space planning can move beyond the confines of past experience to engage with new visions of what the library should be. It does this by exploring what motivated academic library projects in the 1990s and how the building activity of that decade responded to some key academic needs as well as to the traditional operational needs of libraries.

Another book on library architecture notes that "librarianship may be the only profession that derives its name from a particular type of building, the library, which in turn derives its name from a particular physical object, the book. Quite literally, a librarian is one who takes care of books in a building designed to store them. Physicians and nurses are not hospitalians; attorneys are not courtians; and teachers are not schoolians. But librarians are, well, librarians"(Crosbie and Hickey 2001, 6)[*] The effort of this report is to get beyond the literal obligation of libraries described here to a more powerful understanding of the responsibility that librarians, along with others who care deeply about libraries, have to make library buildings fit homes for the learning and teaching processes by which knowledge moves between people and its embodiment in printed books and in fleeting electronic digits.

This report is organized in four parts:

- Part 1 interprets the key findings of the research on which the report is based. This section observes that in the 1990s, higher education saw transformative changes in student learning, faculty teaching methods, and information technology. These changes prompted some responses in library space planning over the last decade, but in many respects the libraries designed in the 1990s were not fundamentally different in concept from those designed in the 1960s. There are good reasons why this should be so, but those reasons obscure two important issues: (1) a bias in library space planning that favors the provision of library services at the expense of the social identity of learning and of knowledge; and (2) a fractured responsibility within the campus community for library space planning, which works against planning that is responsive to the institution's fundamental educational goals.
- Part 2 presents the research data of the study in as neutral an interpretative environment as possible. This is done to enable readers to appraise these data independently of the interpretative essay in part 1.
- Part 3 describes the research methodologies used in the study. Its purpose is to enable readers to judge how reliable the study's findings are and to explore further the implications of the study data.
- Part 4 presents a highly selective, annotated list of readings on library space planning. The list is meant to suggest the range and character of available publications and to point the readers of this report to other useful material.

---

[*] It now appears that some doctors are called "hospitalists"—i.e., doctors that treat patients while they are in the hospital, instead of the patient's primary care physician or the specialist that performed an operation.

PART 1:
LIBRARIES DESIGNED FOR LEARNING

1. Planning Library Space to Advance Learning and Teaching

The 1990s were good years for higher education in the United States and for academic libraries. This was evident not least in the huge investments made in the renovation and expansion of existing libraries and in the construction of new libraries. Between 1992 and 2001, the higher education community spent on average some $449 million annually on library construction. On average, about 2,874,000 gross square feet of space were renovated or built annually.

"I think that libraries have tried to support learning, but I don't think libraries have traditionally said 'We want to make learning happen here.'"
Jill Gremmels, College Librarian, Wartburg College

At the same time that colleges and universities were making these impressive long-term investments in their libraries, they were experiencing at least two fundamental discontinuities with their past. A long-gathering understanding of students' most effective learning behaviors was making itself felt in the adoption of active learning practices. Students everywhere were increasingly working in collaborative study groups of their own making, to engage more strongly and often more adventurously with their coursework. Recognizing the power of this mode of learning, many faculty members built experiential and problem solving materials into their courses and shaped assignments around the expectation of collaborative study. In these and other ways, the daily practices of learning and teaching saw widespread, fundamental change. Quietly but powerfully, American higher education acknowledged and began to engage with the social dimensions of learning and of knowledge.[1]

---

[1] See, for example, Bruffee 1999. Bruffee holds what he describes as a non-foundational view of knowledge, where "knowledge is a community project. People construct knowledge working together in groups, interdependently. All knowledge is therefore the 'property' not of an individual person but of some community or other, the community that constructed it in the language spoken by the members of that community" (p. 294–295). "Collaborative learning makes the Kuhnian assumption that knowledge is a consensus; it is something people construct interdependently by talking together. Knowledge in that sense, Kuhn says, is 'intrinsically the common property of a group or else

The second fundamental change, a revolution in information technology, was not at all quiet and was even more pervasive. While the pace of technological change has steadily accelerated since the 1960s, arguably the "take off" point came with the introduction of the World Wide Web in 1993. The Web in just a few short years gave everyone a reason to connect to the Internet and made connection relatively easy. By the end of the 1990s, information in the developed part of the world was networked. The impact on research and on libraries was profound.[2] Complementary changes in teaching and learning were not slow to follow, not least because each year's freshman class brought students to campus with ever-increasing facility with computing and heightened expectations that information technology would be a central feature of their education.[3]

The question this essay addresses is, "How did space planning for academic libraries during the 1990s address these fundamental changes in American colleges and universities?" In essence, this is a question about two quite legitimate conceptions of the library as a place. One of these, which has a long and worthy tradition, conceives of libraries as service places where information is held, organized, and managed on behalf of those who use it, who are often also directly assisted in their use of information by library staff. The other, which springs from a recognition of the essential social dimension of knowledge and learning,[4] conceives of libraries as spaces where learning is the primary activity and where the focus is on facilitating the social exchanges through which information is transformed into the knowledge of some person or group of persons.

One can investigate the library spaces actually built or renovated in the 1990s to see what balance was struck between these two con-

---

nothing at all'" (p. 133). For the potential impact on libraries of newly adopted pedagogies, see James Wilkinson, "Homesteading on the Electronic Frontier: Technology, Libraries, and Learning," in Dowler 1997, 181–196.

[2] See, for instance, Peter Lyman's essay arguing that scholarly communication was in crisis at the beginning of the 1990s, a crisis that required a fundamental rethinking of the place and function of libraries: "The Library of the (Not-So-Distant) Future," *Change*, 23 (January/February 1991), 31–41. For a broad view of libraries nearly a decade later, see "Digital Revolution, Library Evolution," chapter 1, in *LC21: A Digital Strategy for the Library of Congress*, Committee on an Information Technology Strategy for the Library of Congress, Computer Science and Telecommunications Board, National Research Council (Washington, D.C.: National Academy Press, 2000), 23–49.

[3] For one response to the changing environment for teaching and learning, see the Center for Academic Transformation at Rensselaer Polytechnic Institute, led by Carol A. Twigg. The Center at http://www.center.rpi.edu/ "serves as a source of expertise and support for those in higher education who wish to take advantage of the capabilities of information technology to transform their academic practices." It has published an instructive online newsletter, *The Learning MarketSpace*, available at http://www.center.rpi.edu/PewNews1.html. See also R. J. Thompson, Jr., and L. W. Willard, "Duke University: An Agenda for Institutional Change," in Janet Stocks and Linda R. Kauffman, eds., *Reinvigorating the Undergraduate Experience through Research and Inquiry Based Learning* (Washington, DC: Council for Undergraduate Research, 2003; in press). For an effort to measure systematically some dimensions of active and collaborative learning, see the National Survey of Scholarly Engagement at http://www.indiana.edu/~nsse/.

[4] See, for instance, Bruno Latour and Steve Woolgar, *Laboratory Life: The Social Construction of Scientific Facts* (Beverly Hills: Sage, 1979), and John Seely Brown and Paul Duguid, *The Social Life of Information* (Boston: Harvard Business School Press, 2000).

cepts of library space over the last decade. But in many ways, the space planning process itself—especially its earliest phases, where decisions are made about how a library project will be shaped so as to advance fundamental institutional concerns with learning and teaching—is even more informative. It is here that balancing decisions are made, consciously or not, governing how multi-million dollar investments in library space will focus on library services and on broader, institution-wide agendas in education. This essay describes the kinds of library spaces that emerged in the 1990s to respond to fundamental changes in learning modes and information technology. It also describes the planning processes typical of library projects and argues that higher education is missing opportunities to assert the community-wide ownership of library planning necessary for making new investments in library space highly productive for learning and teaching.

This essay also attempts both to understand the extent to which library planning has been conservative in concept, shaping our response to the future by extrapolating from past experience, and to identify key opportunities to interpose fresh visions of libraries that might produce space design decisions quite different from those of the past. Why does thinking "within the box" serve so well in the design of academic library space, and how might "thinking outside the box" serve even better?

A brief story may suggest the importance of the focus proposed for this essay. The provost of a European university was visiting parts of the United States in 2001, garnering ideas for the construction of a major new library building. The provost included Yale University in these visits and spoke with librarians there about their efforts to focus library space planning on student learning behaviors. The Yale librarians were attempting to design not an information commons, but something called a *learning commons*. The visiting provost immediately saw the point of the learning commons and said with some chagrin how little library planning at her own institution had been informed by thinking about student learning. The chagrin came from the fact that the provost's disciplinary expertise was in education.

Clearly, the weight of traditional thinking about libraries at this provost's university—and at many institutions in the United States— keeps planning focused not on the educational impact but on the service operations of libraries. Traditionally, library buildings are places where we shelve material, circulate things to readers, assist readers with questions about information resources, create instruments such as the catalog for navigating information, and teach readers how to master the complexities of both printed and networked information. Libraries also provide reading accommodations, but historically these accommodations are vulnerable to competing service functions of library space, particularly the need to shelve library materials. Library after library has sacrificed reader accommodations to the imperatives of shelving. The crowding out of readers by reading matter is one of the most common and disturbing ironies in library space planning.[5] These outcomes must be acknowledged, in fact, to be a failure in planning. Such failures are the result of what the visiting provost saw so clearly: close attention in library space planning to library operations and unfocused attention—or outright inattention—to the learning modes of students and the teaching behaviors of faculty. This essay argues that as long as the accommodation of reader needs is narrowly conceived and secondary to provisions for library service operations, the full value of higher education's investments in library space will go unrealized.

2. Level of and Motivations for Investment in Library Space

Writing in 1996, James Neal predicted that colleges and universities would increasingly direct limited capital funds to the renovation of existing library space and would avoid massive investments in new library space.[6] This prediction sensibly reflected the keen competition for campus capital funds, the good economies to be secured through renovation, the diminishing emphasis in many libraries on technical services and the space they require, and—most importantly—the requirements of information technology for virtual rather than physical space.

It turns out that this eminently sensible prediction was wrong. What actually happened between 1992 and 2001 was a substantial and consistent level of investment in library space, year after year. As indicated in Figure 1, each year during this decade saw, on average, some 38 library projects completed. Taken together, these projects cost an annual average of $449 million (in 2001 dollars) and involved on average some 2.9 million gross square feet of space. Of this, new construction accounted for an average of 1.1 million gross square feet, or about 40% of the total space involved.[7] There was no trend, either up or down over the decade, in this percentage of new construction. There was considerable variation in all of these averages from year to year, but the variations fell well within the range of a normal distribution of values.

In addition to spending nearly $4.5 billion on renovating or building new library space during the 1990s, the higher education community incurred substantial new costs for operating and main-

---

5 In the "Defining the Building Problem" section of *Planning Academic and Research Library Buildings*, Leighton and Weber comment that "a shortage of reader space is less likely to be compelling [to those who must set priorities and pay for campus capital projects], even though in educational terms it is as important for effective library use as adequate book or staff space. The consequence of students being forced to seek alternative libraries or to use classrooms or residence rooms for study is not easily determined" (p. 12). The inability to see such consequences has all too often ensured that traditional operational needs of libraries prevail over reader needs when a choice between them had to be made.

6 See James G. Neal, "Academic Libraries: 2000 and Beyond." *Library Journal* 121 (July 1996), 74–76.

7 These annual averages are understated for two reasons. First, the colleges and universities contributing data to the *Library Journal* sometimes do not report project costs. Second, community colleges are significantly under-represented in the *Library Journal* data (see Table 1).

FIGURE 1: INVESTMENT IN LIBRARY SPACE, 1992–2001
Source: *Library Journal* (Table 1)

	Project No.	Total Real $ Cost	Total GSF	New GSF
Annual Average	**37.9**	**$449,453,000**	**2,873,559**	**1,130,872**
Standard deviation	*8.1*	*$159,030,000*	*816,834*	*386,986*

taining that space. Putting operation and maintenance costs at $8 per square foot of space, and disregarding any increased costs associated with renovated space, the cost of operating new academic library space alone on average required at least an additional $9 million every year. These costs cumulate, so that by 2001 higher education had incorporated about $90.5 million of new operating costs into its budgets.

By these measures, there was nothing in the 1990s to indicate any slowing in new investment in academic library space. The age-old truth about libraries—that they always grow in size and demand more space—remained fully in force. It is hard to find evidence that breathtaking innovation in information technology and the "virtual space" it occupies slowed traditional investment in library bricks and mortar.

What motivated this consistently substantial, decade-long investment in new and renovated library space?

A survey of library directors at the institutions making these investments asked this question. Situations at individual colleges and universities varied substantially, and several different motivators were frequently in play at each institution. But five factors, summarized in Figure 2,[8] emerged as clearly most important for colleges and universities considered as a whole.

FIGURE 2: STRONGEST PROJECT MOTIVATORS
Source: CLIR Survey (Table 3a)

Factor	% Projects Strongly Motivated	± confidence interval
Growth of the collections	**57%**	**6%**
Changing character of student study space needs	**45%**	**6%**
Dysfunctional design of previous space	**40%**	**6%**
Changes in or growth of library instruction programs	**32%**	**6%**
Changes in public services other than reference	**26%**	**6%**

Predicted frequency in random distribution = 17%

[8] Figures 2–6 report the percentage of survey respondents answering in a particular way, along with an accompanying plus-or-minus confidence level also stated as a percentage. So for instance, in Figure 2, 57% of the survey respondents reported that their projects (representing a random sample of the larger population of projects) were strongly motivated by the growth of the collections, and one can be 95% confident that all responses for the larger population of projects would fall between 51% and 63%. Note that the practice of reporting percentages of responses along with a plus-or-minus confidence level is used throughout the text and notes of this report. In addition, Figures 2–6 also report, in italics at the bottom of each figure, the percentage response one would expect in a random distribution of responses. In such a distribution, no one or more responses emerge as dominant among the survey respondents. All of the responses reported in Figures 2–5 vary by statistically significant measures from a random distribution, meaning that these are the dominant responses among survey respondents to the question involved.

Survey respondents were asked to rank the strength of these and other possible project motivators on a six-point scale, with values ranging from "not a motivating factor" to "strong motivating factor." A random distribution of responses would result in a given factor being a strong motivator only 17% of the time. All five factors in Figure 2 vary significantly from a random distribution, the first four occurring as strong motivators about twice or more frequently as one would expect in a random distribution of responses.[9]

Survey respondents also identified a number of possible motivators as not influencing their projects. These are shown in Figure 3:

FIGURE 3: WEAKEST PROJECT MOTIVATORS
Source: CLIR Survey (Table 3a)

Factor	% Projects Not Motivated	± confidence interval
Building structural problems	**50%**	**7%**
Increase in the number of service points	**42%**	**7%**
Growth of library staff	**39%**	**6%**
Building safety issues	**32%**	**6%**
Changes in technical services	**27%**	**6%**

Predicted frequency in random distribution = 17%

Here again, survey respondents identified these as non-motivating factors significantly more often than would have occurred in a random distribution of responses. The first four were identified as non-factors about twice or more frequently as one would expect in a random distribution of responses.

Finally, two factors figured in the survey responses in a bipolar way: i.e., they were both non-factors and strong project motivators almost twice as frequently as one would expect in a random distribution of responses. Figure 4 lists these bipolar motivators:

FIGURE 4: BIPOLAR PROJECT MOTIVATORS
Source: CLIR Survey (Table 3a)

Factor	% Projects Strongly Motivated	± confidence interval	% Projects Not Motivated	± confidence interval
Building mechanical systems obsolescence	**33%**	**7%**	**27%**	**6%**
Need to accommodate non-library operations	**26%**	**6%**	**34%**	**6%**

Predicted total frequency in random distribution = 33%

Judging from the absence of comments associated with many of these factors (e.g., collection growth, mechanical systems obsolescence), respondents regarded them as largely self-explanatory. Responses pertinent to some other factors indicated the particular meaning or application they had in individual projects. See "Accom-

---

[9] A November 2001 survey of library directors and chief academic officers at institutions belonging to the Council of Independent Colleges provides parallel data. Respondents at these generally smaller, tuition-dependent institutions indicated the following functions would have high priority in any new library space they might have: instruction in information literacy (79±8%), student study space (75±9%), and shelving library collections (67±9%). See Table 6b for more information.

modating Improved Library Services" on page 13 for a further description of these motivators.[10]

Aside from the factors described in Figures 2–4, the survey inquired about two other possible motivators: changes in reference service and the preservation of the collections. Responses to these factors approximated a random distribution, indicating that while these factors were important to some projects they were not significant motivators for the projects covered in the survey as a whole. The survey also asked about other possible motivators. Respondents mentioned the provision of improved space for archives and special collections and the influence of accreditation requirements a number of times. It is impossible to apply any statistical measures of significance to these "other" responses.

The factors identified here bear only on library space planning and by no means exhaust the possibility for significant change in libraries. Survey responses to the question about changes in reference service as a project motivator illustrate this point. While there was unquestionably much ferment in the library community's thinking about reference service in the 1990s, it did not figure as a significant motivating factor in library space design, presumably because changes in reference service did not consistently drive new ideas for how reference space should be designed.

How might one understand these strong and weak motivators? If one is looking for factors most likely to motivate extrapolative planning,[11] that is to say factors that embody traditional library operations, they are found in the need to

- accommodate growing library collections
- correct for the dysfunctional design of previous library space
- effect changes in public services other than reference (given that these changes most often aimed at increased efficiency in traditional operations)
- overhaul obsolete mechanical systems

---

[10] The analysis presented here applies to all survey respondents, taken as a whole. When one looks at project motivators sorted by date of project completion or by type of institution (using the Carnegie Foundation for the Advancement of Education classification of higher education institutions), the picture is much more varied and less coherent than that presented here. However, only one of the eleven date-of-completion groups and only two of the eleven Carnegie classification groups in which survey respondents fell had thirty or more institutions in them. The small size of most groups reduces the statistical significance of the variations. Possibly the most significant of these variations is that Doctoral/Research Universities (Extensive) were noticeably less strongly motivated by the need to accommodate collection growth than were other types of institutions. This might result from the noticeable turn to off-campus shelving facilities among these institutions, which generally experience robust collection growth. For more information, see Tables 3b–c and 4b–c, provided in the online version of this report, available at http://www.clir.org/pubs/abstract/pub122abst.html.

[11] Robert C. Heterick and Carol A. Twigg describe the difference between extrapolative and interpolative planning in a pair of essays written for *Educom Review* (January/February 1997) and in their online newsletter, *The Learning MarketSpace* (February 2003). See http://www.educause.edu/pub/er/review/reviewArticles/32160.html and http://www.center.rpi.edu/LForum/LM/Feb03.html.

Factors that might, by contrast, drive interpolative planning—where the focus is on uses of library space that cannot be simply predicted from past patterns of use—were found in the need to

- accommodate the changing character of student study needs
- accommodate changes in or the growth of library instruction programs
- accommodate non-library operations

One may fairly conclude that traditional library needs were very strong motivators for the construction and renovation of American academic libraries in the 1990s.[12] The weight of these traditional library needs will become all the more evident in the next parts of the essay, which consider what was built to satisfy these needs and the planning processes used to act on library space needs.

3. Library Project Responses to Motivating Factors

Accommodating Growing Collections

The survey of library directors did not ask whether additional shelving was actually a feature of their projects. The assumption was that projects in some good measure meet the needs that most strongly motivated them. A number of follow-up phone interviews with the library directors who responded to the survey indicated this assumption was appropriate.

The phone interviews provided information about how library directors and academic officers were thinking about collection growth in the 1990s. They had little choice but to consider this issue, as collections of print material continued to grow, just as publishing output grew.[13] To accommodate this growth, new library construc-

---

[12] Steven M. Foote, an architect with extensive experience with libraries and president of Perry Dean Rogers, reported in 1995 that architects and librarians agree that print collections will continue to dominate libraries, that flexible shelving is essential and that compact shelving will be a feature of every library, that adjacencies must be fluid, and that floor-to-ceiling heights must be generous. Regarding information technology, they agree that it should be accommodated but that it will not reduce library space needs. The modest impact of revolutionary change in information technology is evident as well in the most fundamental thinking about library buildings, according to Foote: "At times, even the most erudite and far-thinking clients cannot overcome their traditional ideas of appropriate library design; classical monumentality has been accepted for libraries for centuries. The competition for the main branch of the Chicago Public Library . . . was a case in point. In the end, that jury rather poignantly selected the winner mainly on the grounds that 'It looked like a library.' The standards and values of the nineteenth century still applied, because no more modern imagery [for the library] has convincingly captured our cultural endorsement." See "An Architect's Perspective on Contemporary Academic Library Design," *Bulletin of the Medical Library Association*, 11 (1997), 351.

[13] For instance, the collections at the university libraries that are members of the Association of Research Libraries (ARL) grew by some 94.5 million volumes, or about 29%, in the decade from 1991–1992 through 2000–2001. The number of hardcover books (only) published annually in the United States grew by some 25,000 volumes, or about 90%, in the decade from 1990 to 1999. For information about the growth of library collections, see the annual statistics published by the Association of College and Research Libraries at http://www.ala.org/Content/NavigationMenu/ACRL/Publications/Academic_Library_Statistics/Academic_Library_Statistics.htm, and by ARL at http://www.arl.org/stats/arlstat/index.html. For publishing industry figures, see the yearly statistics published in the *Bowker Annual* (New York: Bowker).

tion and renovation in the 1990s provided shelving space for some 145 million additional volumes, with some 34% of that capacity provided in new construction (see Table 1). Clearly, traditional library needs had a very strong hold on library construction and renovation in the 1990s.

What are the prospects for change regarding this single strongest motivating factor and most traditional of library needs?

None of the 26 library directors interviewed for the study saw electronic publications as offering any relief from the pressure on shelving space as regards monographs, either now or in the foreseeable future. Most did comment, however, that the online availability of journals now offers and will continue to offer appreciable relief from shelving space needs. Library directors regularly commented on their newly acquired ability to remove back files of journals from prime shelving space or from their collections altogether. A number of directors specifically mentioned JSTOR, along with other publishers of electronic journals, as providing this leverage on shelving problems.

Some library directors mentioned designing specialized off-campus shelving facilities, often as a future possibility rather than as a present option for meeting shelving needs. There were probably only three specialized shelving facilities in the study's database of 438 projects undertaken in the 1990s, and only one such facility responded to the survey. It appears from these limited data that the largest research libraries are investing in such facilities and that most of those built in the 1990s were designed for the use of a single institution, rather than as collaborative ventures among a number of institutions.[14] Several directors at libraries with smaller collections expressed the wish to participate, sometime in the future, in a collaboratively managed shelving facility.

For many librarians, the prospect of off-campus facilities remains comfortably in the future; their strong preference for the present is to maintain collections on open, browsable shelving. The facilities manager at one large research library (Interview 11)[15] spoke of having fewer than 10 years of collection growth space, even after a major renovation aimed at providing new compact shelving. He described the pleasure readers take in improved collection access made possible by recent renovations; the relief librarians feel in avoiding off-campus shelving for the present; and a resolve not to assume that such shelving will be the right solution to future shelving problems.

---

14 For information about facilities built collaboratively, see Bernard F. Reilly, Jr., and Barbara DesRosiers, *Developing Print Repositories: Models for Shared Preservation and Access* (Washington, D.C.: Council on Library and Information Resources, 2003). See also Danuta A. Nitecki and Curtis L. Kendrick, eds., *Library Off-site Shelving: Guide for High-Density Facilities* (Englewood, Colo.: Libraries Unlimited, 2001).

15 When individual interviews are referred to in the text of this essay, the kind of institution involved is identified using terms akin to those used by the Carnegie Foundation for the Advancement of Education, and the interview itself (described in part 2 of the report) is referenced. Quoted comments by individuals that are not so referenced come from comments supplied on the survey instrument (described in part 3). Both the interview transcriptions and the survey comments are provided in the online version of this report, available at http://www.clir.org/pubs/abstract/pub122abst.html.

Indeed, a general preference was clear in the interviews for on-site shelving, whether of conventional or movable, high-density design. Most library directors tried to more than meet existing needs with such shelving, some seeking as much as 20 years of additional collection growth space. Though all library directors acknowledged the difficulty of predicting future rates of collection growth, none expressed willingness to forgo any of the shelving they could reasonably include in recently completed projects.

With present shelving needs met, most of the library directors interviewed for this study expressed little anxiety about future shelving needs. Few could imagine such needs becoming urgent during their tenure as directors. More important, many felt that—with burgeoning online resources and off-site shelving facilities a possibility—it was unlikely that shelving needs would ever again drive library space design in the way it had in the past. These directors sensed in the relaxing hold of collection growth on space needs some possibility for interpolating new ideas about the use of library space.[16] The ambiguous force of such thinking was, however, evident in the view of one liberal arts college dean (Interview 6) that it was quite possible in the next 20 years for pressure from the college's growing collections to displace reader accommodations, as it had before.

> It certainly could [happen]. It's probably 10 years down the line . . . but I could see that happening. . . . It's just the realities of working within a fairly tight budget. . . . One of the things that happened when we got done with the renovation and expansion is that the space got so much more attractive that the number of visitors [i.e., readers] simply doubled or tripled. It went way, way up. And so the question is, can the library if it gets significantly more full [with print material] still accommodate that number of students? And it will be difficult.

Library directors and chief academic officers alike observed how commonly in the past the need to add shelving crowded readers out of library buildings. In this way, libraries became ever more simply places to house printed collections. When choices were forced, shelving the collections has been more important than maintaining reader accommodations. New construction and renovation are commonly designed to counter—for shorter or longer periods of time—this apparently unstoppable tendency of the collection to consume space and, ironically, to drive readers away from libraries. It is going to take more than a decade of experience with electronic publications and alternative shelving practices to free higher education from the threat that print collections pose to good libraries. There is evidence

---

16 See, for instance, a 1992 account of the study, requested of the Minnesota State University system by the state legislature, to envision the library of the future: Linda Bunnel Jones, "Linking Undergraduate Education and Libraries: Minnesota's Approach," *New Directions for Higher Education*, no. 78 (1992), 27–35. The Minnesota study held that because libraries would, in the future, rely extensively on one another for collection sharing, there would be more space available "to devote to students' learning environments. [The study's architects recommended] a reversal of the ratio of books to study space from the previous 50% for collections and 38% for study space" (p. 33).

that many involved with library planning hope a process of gradual change has moved us past the point where this familiar cycle of behaviors will entrap us again. But there is little evidence that the higher education community has reached the point in its thinking about libraries where it is ready to affirm that readers will assuredly have first claim on space even when space becomes highly constrained by collection growth.

Accommodating Improved Library Services

Library projects in the 1990s were designed to meet a host of operational needs beyond that of shelving collections. As indicated in Figure 2, the single most frequently expressed such need was for space to support the library staff's instructional activities in information literacy and staff development. The need for electronic classrooms has become so apparent that survey respondents felt little need to comment on anything beyond the number, size, technical capabilities, and use policies for such instructional spaces.[17]

Figure 2 also indicates that library projects in the 1990s were strongly motivated by the need to accommodate the delivery of public services other than reference. Survey respondents described numerous public service activities—prominently including circulation, interlibrary loan (ILL), and special collections—that benefited from new or renovated space. The automation of library functions and concomitant changes in workflows were often mentioned as factors that motivated capital projects. Respondent comments suggested renovations rarely reached beyond the operational needs of individual library departments in their consequences. The comment of one doctoral university respondent typifies the description of these operational goals:

> [We wanted] to consolidate access services functions to reduce service points and to better utilize both space and staff. For example, we felt that reserve processing and ILL services should be adjacent to one another to maximize the use of equipment and staff. We envisioned using reserve staff to assist ILL staff in ILL during the summer and during other slow times in course reserve processing. We also envisioned using ILL staff for copying and scanning course reserve materials during Reserves' peak times. We have been able to make these staffing changes work because of the reconfigured spaces.

There was also some need to accommodate non-library operations in library projects. As indicated in Figure 4, such needs produced a bipolar response. Significantly more respondents (25±6%)

---

17 The survey among Council of Independent Colleges institutions confirmed the importance of teaching space for the library's own instructional program. Some 75±8% of those respondents strongly agreed that existing library space should support such activities, while 79±8% of the respondents would assign high priority to such activities in any new library space. There was a statistically significant difference of opinion on this matter between library directors and chief academic officers, of whom 96±4% and 66±9% respectively would give high priority to such activities in new library space (see Tables 6a–b).

than one would expect in a random distribution indicated that the need to accommodate non-library operations was not a factor in their planning, while at the same time significantly more than one would expect (34±6%) indicated it was a strong motivator. Respondents mentioned media services, academic computing services, centers for instructional technology, centers for teaching and learning (often but not necessarily rooted in instructional technology), and student writing centers as academic operations not administered by the library but sometimes housed in library buildings. Interviews with library directors suggested that decisions to place these functions in library buildings were most often simply pragmatic—i.e., library space existed or could be created for these units—rather than a product of strategic collaboration between such units and the library. Strategic partnerships can indeed develop out of the experience of library and other academic staff working in close proximity with one another, but such partnerships seem most often to develop after the fact and slowly.[18]

By far the most common provision for the changing operational needs of libraries was to design for as much flexibility in future uses of space as possible.[19] Some 72±6% of survey respondents said their projects provided for future changes in space use, a figure substantially above what one would expect in a random distribution of responses. Survey respondents frequently mentioned open, modular floor plans, floor loading capability for both conventional and moveable shelving, pervasive conduits for electrical power and telecommunications, and flexibility in providing networking technology as key strategies for meeting future, mostly unpredictable, needs. One respondent at a master's degree institution commented soberly that such flexibility in providing for an unknowable future comes at a cost, and that "budget realities forced us to cut back somewhat on flexibility." Costly as such flexibility may be, the certainty of change makes it a good investment. Some 61±6% of survey respondents reported having experienced the need to make further space changes relatively soon after completing their projects (Table 4a, question

---

[18] The Council of Independent Colleges survey asked specifically about the inclusion in libraries of centers for innovation in teaching and learning. Responses suggest changing views about the desirability of including such activities in library buildings. Only 16±7% of those respondents strongly agreed that existing library space should support such activities, while 30±9% of the respondents would assign high priority to such activities in new library space. There was a statistically significant difference of opinion on this matter between library directors and chief academic officers, of whom 44±10% and 18±8% respectively would give high priority to such space use (see Tables 6a–b).

[19] For an extended treatment of this subject, see Brand 1994. Brand identifies libraries as "a glorious case for study [of what he calls High Road buildings]. They exude architectural permanence. Meanwhile their collections grow and grow, and the pressure [for change] builds" (p. 44). Writing of the Boston Athenaeum and the London Library, Brand says that "the product of careful continuity is love. Members of both libraries adore their buildings. . . . Trust, intimacy, intense use, and time are what made these buildings work so well" (p. 49).

13).[20] Several respondents described the benefits already realized from flexible designs, one of them from a doctoral university saying that "flexibility was a big issue, thus, big open floors not filled with stacks has been a big boon. We have moved services, technology, and collections multiple times since completion [in 2001]."

Beyond specific operational needs, planning for new and renovated library space commonly aimed at accommodating broad shifts in information technology. The comment of one respondent from a master's degree institution explains the importance of such planning:

> [We had] a tremendous need to transform a 1960/1970s facility into a twenty-first century academic library. The library renovation and expansion project was as much about preparing for new technologies as it was about our need for additional space. This gets a #5 [i.e., a strong motivation rating in the survey]!

Survey respondents often commented on efforts to link print and electronic resources by locating workstations in the midst of print collections; to provide readers with ubiquitous connectivity through wired or wireless systems; and to develop information commons that provide workstations with a variety of information management software and access to broad-ranging information resources. Taken together, such efforts could go some distance toward changing a library's authority on campus and its image of itself, as another respondent from a doctoral university made clear in describing the impact of a major consultant's study of information technology:

> That report from an outside group made it possible for the library to have influence that it would not otherwise have had. The campus had made the decision to focus on technology. This provided somewhat of a blueprint. And I think frankly it allowed the library to present a picture that was not entirely dependent on the campus computing center's perspectives, which were probably not as ambitious as were [those] involved in this report. . . . [The report] really changed the nature of the conversation rather than making any specific recommendations. It really positioned the library to be a different thing than it would have been, in the way the whole campus thought about it, rather than the specific projections on the technology. . . .
>
> Importantly, the library went from being a small underfunded library at a second tier university to one of the most technologically sophisticated academic libraries in the country. Over several years the library's conception of itself changed to

[20] One would predict this need to be more evident in projects completed earlier in the 1990s and less evident in projects completed later in the decade. Analysis of the responses by year provides weak support for this hypothesis. The actual distribution of responses on this matter differed significantly from a random distribution for 1994, 1997, and 1998, where the number of positive responses (i.e., responses indicating the need to accommodate further change) was statistically high, and in 2000 and 2001, where the number of positive responses was statistically low.

view itself as a leader. The new building and the technology that came with it in many ways transformed the whole library's view of itself.[21]

The architectural challenges involved in making the changes described here, though surely important, are nonetheless relatively ordinary: attention to adjacencies, the more effective use of space, designing to support efficient workflows, open floor plans, and robust telecommunications capabilities. Success in handling such commonplace design issues can pay remarkable dividends. Library operations become notably more convenient and more efficient for readers and staff alike. Due especially to the capabilities of library management systems and the provision of online information resources, readers are no longer required to visit the library to discover and make effective use of information. They readily command immense library and other information resources in their offices, laboratories, and residence halls, at home, and even on the campus green. Readers have embraced the virtual library and value it highly. In the 1990s, libraries dramatically enhanced their utility by moving much of their services into virtual space and reducing the necessity of using actual library space.[22]

Accommodating Students' Need for Learning Spaces

Libraries succeeded so well in improving their services and supporting electronic information resources that many—especially those asked to pay for it—began to question the need for bricks and mortar library space. The dean of a liberal arts college (Interview 6) wanted particularly to counter the view that libraries as places are becoming obsolete because of the emergence of information technology. He wanted to protect the idea of a traditional library as a vital component in the life of the college. "There are voices out there that would tend to feel that the library is something of an albatross around an institution's neck, and that's not the case at all." Understanding better the behaviors of those who continue to make frequent and significant use of library space, especially students who are by far the most frequent users of library space,[23] and responding to those needs became an important counter to the skepticism voiced about the value of library space.

The dean just quoted argued that the library is "probably the most important place for learning on campus. . . ." Recognizing this

---

21 The last sentence of this quotation comes from the respondent's written comments made on the study's survey; the rest of the quotation is from the respondent's interview (Interview 17).

22 See Scott Carlson, "The Deserted Library: As Students Work Online, Reading Rooms Empty Out—Leading Some Campuses to Add Starbucks," *Chronicle of Higher Education*, November 16, 2001, A35–A38. See also Amy Friedlander, *Dimensions and Use of the Scholarly Information Environment. Introduction to a Data Set Assembled by the Digital Library Federation and Outsell, Inc.* (Washington, D.C.: Digital Library Federation and Council on Library and Information Resources, 2002), part 2: Infrastructure, Facilities, Services, and Table 66, available at http://www.clir.org/pubs/reports/pub110/introduction.html#part2.

23 See Friedlander, part 2 and Table 32.

value, the study survey asked a number of questions about the ways reader accommodations, and especially student accommodations, were improved. These questions were not concerned with the direct operational needs of libraries (for instance, to shelve its collections or improve circulation functions), but with the need to accommodate the learning behaviors of students. These questions were asked to help understand how library design in the 1990s responded to the needs of students not simply as users of information but more broadly as learners.

Asked about student learning spaces, library directors reported providing group study space much more frequently than one would expect in a random distribution of responses (see Table 4a, question 7).[24] Interviews with library directors and academic officers suggested that the need for such space became newly apparent to them during the 1990s, as they consulted with students and observed what succeeded in other library projects. Tellingly, one research library project (completed in 1996) that was strongly oriented toward students nonetheless missed the importance of group study, at least in one respect, and had to reconfigure its space after the fact as student preferences became apparent. The institution's chief academic officer (Interview 1) affirmed that the project was informed by a

> deep conviction . . . that students would drive the evolution of this facility. . . . And for many years, we'd had the philosophy in other parts of the university that you build a very powerful and flexible environment, and then you let the students shape it. So for example, when we first built the place, we built it in the traditional way in which each student would have their own workstation and so forth. And then we began to realize that's not the way students work these days. They work in teams where three or four students will gather round, and they have three or four workstations. So we reconfigured all of that, to let the students define how they learned and how they approached their activities. . . . We felt that if we built the space, and did it in a flexible way, the students would define their own learning environment. I think that's what's been happening.

The library director at another doctoral university (Interview 12) spoke with obvious pleasure of the way his project enables effective student learning:

> Just the most notable thing about usage is . . . the extreme growth in group study. . . . We're seeing that virtually all of [some 250 tables seating four to six students] are filled with students working together, and . . . the thing that makes us happiest is that we somehow stumbled into a really high-use kind of thing here that reflects how people function within their classes and work

---

24 This was also the case in the survey conducted among institutions belonging to the CIC. Of these respondents, 51±10% indicated that accommodations for collaborative learning among students would have high priority in new library space. There was a statistically significant difference of opinion on this matter between library directors and chief academic officers, of whom 64±9% and 41±10% respectively would give high priority to such uses of new library space (see Table 6b).

with their fellow students. . . . [This space] will be filled, literally
every chair, . . . and they're all talking at the same time. And the
hum that rises above this is just amazing. And they don't care. . . .
There's all this din that occurs [from] hundreds of students in this
same space, all working together and all talking at the same time.
Immediately adjacent to a typical space like this is a space with
like 60 computers, and they're all clustered around the computers
as well, working together in some cases. Somehow it just all
came together as a very useful space for students. . . . We just
beam with pride. Every time I come down the elevator to leave,
and I see these hundreds of students out there—that just never
happened before.

Group study space was the only kind of student accommodation
that respondents mentioned more often than would occur in a random distribution of responses. Other student-oriented spaces (e.g.,
computing laboratories,[25] conference or other information meeting
space) did, however, figure in the responses, as did traditional ways
of meeting student study needs, such as carrels and general purpose
or subject- or format-specialized reading rooms. Several respondents
described accommodations provided for students with disabilities.
One library director at a master's degree institution emphasized
the need to accommodate a variety of student learning modes: "We
pride ourselves on creating as many different study environments as
there are 'study styles.' Large and open, small and intimate, lots of
sunlight, low light, etc. etc."

Two other kinds of space directly responsive to student needs
deserve mention here: space for social purposes and for food. The
view that food should be kept out of libraries seems largely to have
collapsed in the 1990s. Survey respondents reported that 50±9% of
the projects included vending machine food and beverages, while
23±8% reported including staffed food services and another 27±8%
reported some other type of food service. The provision of vended
food occurs more often than one would expect in a random distribution of responses (see Table 4a, question 9). It would seem that new
library construction or renovation now regularly provides some kind
of food service. This surely responds to student desires (often expressed in defiance of library rules against food and beverages) and
to the practices of some bookstores. If one acknowledges the social
dimensions of learning and knowledge, the provision of food—so
often strongly associated with social activities—seems quite appropriate. One respondent at a doctoral university commented on the
extraordinary success of its library's food service:

Three years ago . . . the library built a donor-funded café
serving beverages, espresso, sandwiches, pastries, and grilled
sandwiches. The café is open 90 hours a week and 24 hours [a

---

[25] Most respondents to the survey among CIC institutions assigned only medium
priority to general computing laboratories for students as a feature of new
library space. Statistically, the responses to this question approximated a random
distribution, so it cannot be said that respondents were decidedly of one view
about how important such a facility would be in new library space (see Table 6b).

day] during finals. An outside vendor is operating the [café name]. The café is proving to be the most successful on-campus food operation.

The social dimensions of learning and knowledge found many other architectural expressions in projects of the 1990s. Survey respondents frequently described entrance lobbies and atria, group study rooms and other study areas, computer laboratories, and lounges as social space. Other responses indicate a wide variety of spaces (from elevator lobbies to rooftop gardens) are used as social space. Several respondents mentioned outdoor spaces adjacent to the library as having been built and landscaped explicitly as social spaces. It is clear that students will create social spaces for themselves, whether or not space is designed for this purpose. A respondent at a doctoral university commented that "in the old library, social groups making noise were disruptive so this activity was designed out of the new building. The students of course found their own way to socialize and noise is an issue." Another respondent at a master's degree university happily affirmed that "I consider the entire facility a social space for students." Still another respondent at a doctoral university reported that "fortunately or un[fortunately], the entire library has become a huge social space. Our usage is soaring, it is hard to find a seat at many times, and we are a most popular destination for our students."

This last comment suggests some ambivalence about the library being so popular a social space among students. Statistically, survey respondents reported providing social spaces for students some 47±7% of the time, close to what one would see in a random distribution of responses. Ambivalence about concepts of the library as a place for individual and for social study is more evident in a separate survey, conducted in November 2001 among library directors and chief academic officers at institutions belonging to the CIC (see Tables 6a and 6b). Respondents at these typically smaller, tuition-dependent institutions agreed strongly only 16±7% of the time that socializing among students (without food service) should have high priority in *existing* library space. This view was expressed much less often than one would expect in a random distribution of responses. The same respondents, however, assigned high priority 26±8% of the time to such socializing space in any *new* library space that might be created on their campuses. And while most of these respondents (41±10%) gave social space only medium priority, the upward shift in priority for the social uses of existing and new library space may suggest a growing acceptance of the importance of the social dimensions of learning and knowledge.

Thinking about the library as a social space, rather than as space primarily for undisturbed reading and individual study, involves some recasting of ideas about what makes for success in library planning. The importance to students of this recasting was strikingly evident at one liberal arts college, where the library director (Interview 25) reported there had been no place on campus for students to study together, except the dormitories, which did not work well. Students, he said, were sitting on hallway floors and in vacant classrooms. They "wanted to come together in some other place, and in fact they do come together now [at the library]. This is both a very social and a very studious library. . . . . And it's been that way since we opened up." In their behavior, students at this college and elsewhere have affirmed quite decidedly there is no contradiction in thinking of the library as both a social and a studious place.[26]

4. Project Planning Methods

Recognizing the importance of the initial steps in project planning, institutions engaged seriously with various assessment, goal-setting, and programming activities. Significant variation in these activities is, however, apparent. One respondent at a general baccalaureate college commented that "we had done . . . [assessment] activities as a matter of course," while another respondent at a doctoral university reported that "very little time [was] given to assessment, due to the press of work and the small number of staff members." A number of respondents distanced themselves from the survey's emphasis on *systematic* assessment by describing their planning as "thorough" or "extensive," if not "systematic." This comment from the library director at a doctoral university typified such caveats:

> While we could not claim to having done formal assessments, we certainly spent time analyzing not only the present but also the future trends in student learning, teaching, and . . . learning spaces and learning technologies. Our goal was to be ahead of the curve and proactive—not just a responder.

Follow-up interviews with library directors made it clear how informal many assessment activities were.

Figure 5 lists the planning methods survey respondents reported using significantly more often than one would expect in a random distribution of responses.

FIGURE 5: FREQUENTLY USED PLANNING METHODS
Source: CLIR Survey (Table 4a)

Planning method	% of affirmative responses	± confidence interval
Systematic assessment of library operations	85%	5%
Faculty involvement in planning	75%	6%
Project influenced by overall "vision" statement	65%	6%
Systematic assessment of reader or user wishes	64%	6%
Systematic assessment of fit with other spaces	58%	7%

Predicted frequency in random distribution = 50%

By far the most frequent planning method was the assessment of library operations. Survey respondents describe surveying faculty and student opinion about operations, projecting collection growth, identifying appropriate environmental standards for preserving collections, studying adjacencies, and doing environmental

---

[26] Another library director, serving at a doctoral university (Interview 8), observed that "the library is one of the few places on campus where you can be productive and social at the same time."

scans—especially of information technology. These assessments were sometimes done by or with the assistance of a library consultant. Site visits to other libraries, reference to library space standards set by the Association of College and Research Libraries (ACRL), and statistical comparisons with peer institutions were also mentioned as means of systematic assessment.

To meet needs without wasteful duplication, library projects were often planned with reference to other spaces available on campus, especially student gathering spaces, auditoriums, and computer laboratories. Survey respondents reported planning the library as an element in a larger plan of campus accommodations 58±7% of the time, a rate that differs just slightly from what one would expect in a random distribution of responses.

As Figure 5 indicates, faculty were regularly involved, especially in the preliminary stages of planning, when project goals were determined. Commonly, such involvement was achieved through standing library advisory committees or committees appointed especially for the building project. Normally, students served on these committees as well, but their involvement appears to be less certain and their impact less significant. Some 51±7% of the respondents reported students being involved in space planning, a rate indistinguishable from a random distribution of responses.[27] Many survey comments indicate that faculty and student views had little impact on the planning process; no comments identified faculty or students as having a major impact. One librarian at a liberal arts college (Interview 26) commented that both faculty and student representatives on the project planning committee showed little significant interest in detailed planning, attending meetings only when the architect made presentations. The role of faculty in library planning is described more fully in section 7.

Some 65±6% of survey respondents reported that their projects were meaningfully influenced by an overall vision statement describing the library's mission and services. These documents are typically the products of substantial planning exercises that can be either independent of library space planning or integral to it. Vision statements commonly serve to explain and validate the library's mission and win broad adherence to that mission within the academic community.[28] In actuality, by far the most important audience for such statements is the library staff that develops them. Other audiences include the faculty and student committee that commonly advises the library director, the administrative officer to whom the library reports, and—where appropriate—those charged with space planning.

While vision statements typically assert the centrality of libraries to academic life and the role libraries play in supporting teaching and learning, these statements are rarely informed by any systematic

---

[27] The same percentage of respondents reported consulting with still other constituencies, including institutional governing boards, alumni, community members, donors, and Library Friends.

[28] See, for instance, Jo McClamroch, Jacqueline J. Byrd, and Steven L. Sowell, "Strategic Planning: Politics, Leadership, and Learning," *Journal of Academic Librarianship*, 27 (2001), 372–378.

assessment of how students actually learn or how faculty teach. The same is true of space planning. Figure 6 lists the planning methods respondents reported using significantly less often that one would expect in a random distribution of responses.

FIGURE 6: INFREQUENTLY USED PLANNING METHODS
Source: CLIR Survey (Table 4a)

Planning method	% of affirmative responses	± confidence interval
Systematic assessment of modes of student learning	41%	6%
Systematic assessment of modes of faculty teaching	31%	6%
Post-occupancy assessment	16%	5%

Predicted frequency in random distribution = 50%

It is regrettable that library claims to support learning and teaching are so rarely backed by any formal, systematic understanding of these most fundamental activities of higher education. Interviews with library directors made clear that even when, in the survey, the director had affirmed doing a systematic assessment of student modes of learning, what had typically been done was a survey of student preferences regarding group study space and types of seating.

Although it spends hundreds of millions of dollars every year on building and renovating library space, the academic community in America rarely feels the need, as Figure 6 indicates, to undertake any formal post-occupancy study of the success of library projects.[29] No doubt the daily experience of working in and of serving readers in new or renovated space provides telling evidence about project success. And library directors are not slow to recognize the need for further change. As noted on page 14, some 61±6% of survey respondents reported the need to make further changes in their libraries relatively soon after the completion of their projects (see Table 4a, question 13). The data most commonly cited to support claims of project success are counts of people entering the library. These and library circulation figures often increase dramatically after the completion of a library project.[30] These figures often match campus-wide changes in the perception of the library as an object of institutional pride and as a prized means of advancing teaching and learning. The library director at a master's degree institution (Interview 21) proudly reported that "one faculty member said to me, . . . this [renovation of the library] is the best thing to happen to students on our campus in 30 years. And I think that's absolutely true."

---

[29] For an exception to this practice, see Lynda H. Schneekloth and Ellen Bruce Keable, "Evaluation of Library Facilities: A Tool for Managing Change," *Occasional Papers*, University of Illinois Graduate School of Library and Information Science, Number 191, November 1991.

[30] See, for instance, Harold B. Shill and Shawn Tonner, "Does the Building Really Matter? Facility Improvements and Academic Library Usage," contributed paper, ACRL 11th National Conference, Charlotte, N.C., April 12, 2003. PowerPoint slides are available at http://www.hbg.psu.edu/library/presentations.html.

5. Character of Planning Methods and their Outcomes

Was library space planning in the 1990s still primarily extrapolating on past experience, in the belief that the only prediction about the future that could confidently be made was that it would look rather like the past? Or was planning in some way attempting to interpolate a significantly different vision of the future and hoping to bring that future into being through planning decisions?

It appears from the survey data that library space planning was still primarily extrapolative, responding strongly to traditional needs and ideas of library service.[31] To test this perception, the following proposition and questions were put to the library directors interviewed for this study:

> Survey results indicate that while changes in technology frequently drive the need to reconfigure library space for specific services and operations, there is relatively little fundamental rethinking of the need for and uses of library space. Aside from the omnipresent computer (often presented in clusters), group study space, and electronic classrooms, library space today has much the same character and basic function as library space built a generation ago.
> • Do you agree with this characterization of your project? If not, how would you modify it?
> • Should we expect major changes in library space design to evolve in largely incremental and experimental ways, building on what we know has worked well in the past?
> • Are there opportunities to break with an evolutionary process of library design and adopt more radical, revolutionary, and possibly risky views of what library space should be?

The phone interviews did not always adhere closely to their script, with the result that only 21 of the 25 library directors (84%) interviewed were asked these questions, and of them 19 (76%) responded in ways that were directly pertinent.

Nine library directors affirmed that the projects they had helped to plan were intentionally aimed at traditional needs and designed to affirm the traditional identity of the library. Seven others offered "Yes, but . . ." answers, saying that the proposition fit their library project, with only some qualification. Only two library directors described their projects as aiming at and achieving some fundamentally different vision of the library. One respondent (Interview 14) reported that efforts to reconceive the library as a "teaching library" had failed. Staff members were not enthusiastic about the idea and were glad to see this emphasis die with the departure of the library director who advocated it. "Looking back on these efforts, they now seem linear—i.e., as reasonable and predictable lines of evolutionary development. At the

---

[31] The library director at a doctoral university (Interview 17) described his project in a way that makes clear how little impact on the physical building a design intended to be pace-setting in technology can be: "In a lot of ways, the building is a very traditional library structure. . . . They just put a lot of wire and a lot of technological capability into a structure that is largely a very traditional building."

time (very early 1990s), they looked more revolutionary."

Those affirming traditional purposes in planning were clear about the values they hoped to achieve. The library director at one master's degree institution (Interview 20) said:

> We built a very traditional building. We sought to provide comfort, quiet, light . . . and convenience—and that's what was missing in the old building. A lack of comfort, I think, if I could sum it up in one word. It just wasn't attractive, it didn't feel good to come in; people used to tell us they were doing fine until they got an assignment that made them come into the library. . . . Our design has worked magnificently. And we get compliments constantly about the way the building feels when they come in. [So we] satisfied some basic human need for comfortable space to sit, to focus and concentrate. . . . I also see faculty who actually come . . . [to] hide out over here. Never did that before! So we're meeting a need for things other than the computers and wireless networks and group study and conference rooms.

Another director, at a liberal arts college (Interview 25), made the same point, emphasizing the communal function of the library:

> Libraries are [often] very gloomy; they're not very nice places. They're not attractive. . . . Why shouldn't students have decent light and a comfortable chair and a clean environment and room to spread out their materials so they can work? And also to be able to see their friends when they're there? You know, this is their community now. They've left home; this is their world. And so I think that's what we're providing them: a place where they can develop and grow.

Another director, at a doctoral university (Interview 9), described the effort to design the library as a campus crossroads, open to a variety of activities not managed by the library, as aimed at traditional values. "We're designing to functions that I hope will still be embedded in the library of the future, in terms of intellectual and social commons for students and faculty." One other director, at another master's degree institution serving one of the nation's largest cities, described the result of providing readers with library space that is both comfortable and handsome:

> The building is so unbelievably gorgeous, and so majestic; it's so grand. . . . If you came to our building, I'm sure you would be in awe. It is like what a grand, wonderful library should be. . . . It has an impact on what people do when they're in the building, how they feel. . . . It's a very important statement for the college to make. It's the most democratic building on campus, and if it's grand and awe inspiring and at the same time warm, comfortable, and inviting, it makes a tremendous statement about how the college feels about learning and teaching. Our president has said that for [the institution's name,] the library is an article of faith.

Notably, these champions of the traditional library speak compellingly about reader accommodation. While survey results indicate that accommodating print collections was the single most powerful project motivator in the 1990s (see Figure 2), it is reader accommodation that seems most powerfully to define the traditional library.

Most of the library directors who responded with "Yes, but . . ." comments qualified their affirmation of traditional purposes by describing efforts to provide supportive environments for the use of information technology. Actual changes in library spaces focused on computer clusters, information commons, and decisions about adjacencies between print collections and computers. Two institutions reported diametrically opposite results in bringing print and electronic resources into close proximity, one having to abandon the effort after the original project design proved a failure. The director at a regional campus of a doctoral university commented that while no effort was made to design a radically different library, and while conservative attitudes among some faculty inhibit radical change, it is nonetheless possible to advance significant change: "If we infuse technology into library space, we affect perceptions of people in the environment. We position the library in a way that it can be seen as a leader in the intelligent adoption of technology for use within the community." The effort here is to change perceptions not of library space but of the library as an organization.

A librarian at a liberal arts college (Interview 28) described the first phase of their renovations as aimed at traditional needs, while the current phase pursues a significantly different view of the use of library space:

> We are changing with this renovation from an old fashioned library where the client comes in and consults with the librarian or consults with a computer to get some information and then goes off to do whatever they're going to do. What we are planning for and implementing right now is space that supports a student who comes in and wants to start her research in the reference area. So she sits down at a spacious table with a computer. She spreads herself out and she goes to work. She does her work. She starts her writing. She talks with a reference librarian and so on. So she's there for the duration. . . . Just a few steps away is a very large reading room. And this really defines the change too. Before the renovation it had been stack area. . . . After the renovation, . . . this area is becoming a large reading room which is going to have vending machines with it so that students can go in and relax a little bit, can eat, can do their work, and at the other end of the room they have newspapers and current periodicals. So while the standard resources are still here, the way we allot the space and place our service points has evolved.

The interviews suggested some experimentation in designing space to support readers deeply engaged with electronic information resources. The library director at a doctoral university (Interview 13) described the uncertainty and the importance of such planning, given the amounts being invested in library and other buildings:

What we're trying to do is to figure out the physical requirements, the space requirements . . . [for] the new role we see the library playing in terms of the creation and management of digital information. The need to educate and train students and faculty on use of the technology and the ways of creating new digital products are all things that we're trying to think through in terms of space requirements in the new library. We don't have the answers there, and we haven't found anyone who has the answers. The architects aren't helpful, because it's not an area where they've had a whole lot of experience. What you describe [i.e., traditional library design] is exactly what we see around us in terms of how other people have gone about thinking about the technology piece of what they're doing. And we're looking for some better support, some better advice. It's part of a larger campus problem that I've identified here everywhere. There's a tremendous amount of construction going on on this campus right now, compensating for 20 years of neglect on academic facilities. And there is such a huge disconnect between the architecture—the design of the space—and the technology piece. Those two pieces have not been brought together.

Vital as the effective accommodation of information technology is, it arguably should not be the dominant concern in planning new library space. The library director at a liberal arts college commented, in a follow-up message after the interview, that

there is a strange dialectic right now (at least since the mid-1990s) between libraries and technology that we in the profession have not worked through. I['m] thinking here not just of the print/electronic nexus but also the notion of a library as a space for thought, reflection, study, and active learning. . . . In planning new spaces, we should have . . . [this second set of issues] foremost in our minds. But it's hard, because many on our campuses really just want us to solve [i.e., eliminate] the 'space problem' rather than begin the process of rethinking the role of the library in positive, proactive way.

The same library director (Interview 29) commented that technology sometimes drives library design for the worse, producing libraries that are over-designed for technology. "Technology was not the solution to our problem, and we really need to let the teaching mission drive the process. So we listened closely to the faculty, and we tried to listen to students."

Only two library directors reported success in a significant re-conceptualization of the library.[32] In one case, at a doctoral university, this was the result of the chief academic officer's leadership and

---

32 The William H. Welch Medical Library at Johns Hopkins University was not in the database of projects developed for this study. But recent planning for this library is notable for its interpolative re-visioning of how library space might be used. Nancy Roderer, director of the Welch Library, wrote in private communication with the author that Welch Library staff "imagined that [in the future] the medical information user's everyday information needs could all be met electronically—and then tried to work backwards to the current time." The summary report on this planning may be read at http://www.welch.jhu.edu/architecturalstudy/summary/summary.pdf.

his insistence on the value of proximity and integration among information resource units. This person—described by the library director as the "godfather" and "guardian angel" of the project (Interview 8)—insisted that the library and other technology units share the building without having their own discrete spaces.

> In the planning process for this building, . . . the library was uncomfortable with basically being in a building that had such a large non-library presence, and probably felt a little threatened by that, and at one point said, 'Well, just give us our space, and we'll take care of designing that; you [other] guys can go do whatever you want to do.' And that clearly was not going to be the way this was approached. It wasn't until the library gave that up—and a lot of preconceptions were dropped by everybody, really—that things became much more integrated.

The result was that "space in the building was designed to be shared," making it imperative that people from different disciplines and different administrative units work "side-by-side." The result is that one often cannot tell what physical space "belongs" to what program. The library director exemplified the benefits of these arrangements by describing the interaction of library staff with another unit's software evaluation staff: "Proximity is, of course, the thing that really does it more than anything else. Proximity to the special things that exist in this building as well as proximity to the other staff." The chief academic officer (Interview 1) described the building as a "creative space, built around creativity and technology" and speculated that "when the building finally came on line . . . my suspicion was that there probably weren't over a dozen people in the university that had the foggiest idea what it was." Significantly, the building has been immensely successful with students but has had uncertain success among faculty:

> Part of the challenge is to get the faculty comfortable with coming in to this non-traditional kind of space. Students have no problem with it; they take to it like ducks take to water. They walk in, and within half an hour have found what they need. . . . They navigate very easily. Faculty are very intimidated, particularly because there are so many students in the building all times of the day and night. So we haven't quite figured out how to get faculty here and engaged in it, and by faculty I also mean faculty bringing in their graduate student research teams. And I'm not quite sure what we need to do with that yet. . . . We may try some experiments.

The other library director who described an intention to counter traditional values in planning her library serves at a general baccalaureate college (Interview 31). She described her planning as follows:

> We didn't start out with what I think is the traditional question, 'How much stuff do we have to get in this building and what kind of stuff is it?' . . . We didn't do that. We started out the planning by saying. 'What do we want to happen in this

building?' And the answer to that was that we wanted to be much more proactive about promoting learning. . . . And that's what we were trying to do—both information literacy, which we consider our discipline, but also other kinds of learning—and we wanted the architecture to make it be like a think tank atmosphere, where there would be lots of exciting ideas bouncing around, and people could interact with each other and text and whatever technological stuff they might require, so that great minds could do their thing in this space.

This library director described a planning session with an architect, a consultant, the college dean, a faculty member, two regents, and an information technology specialist as

an amazing experience. And that's when we came up with the whole notion that we have three things coming together in this building: we have learners, experts, and tools. And this is the only place where that particular combination comes [together]. Tools you can get anywhere now, and learners can be anywhere and should be anywhere. But experts are not quite so mobile—both librarian experts and classroom faculty experts. But where we all come together is right here in this library.

It was far from clear how best to design space to exploit what makes the library unique on campus:

We tried to find literature about the design of educational spaces . . . . I was amazed; I found next to nothing, and I thought surely school designers must think about these things, don't they? But I couldn't find anything. I was trying to find out more things about learning styles. We knew we wanted to accommodate many different kinds of learning styles here. . . . But we didn't have a lot of guidance from anything except our own sense as learners and teachers of what people might need. We hoped if we provided enough different kinds of spaces, people would find ones that were convenient for them, or conducive to their own styles.

The library director described herself and her colleagues not as information "handmaidens," waiting for readers to ask for help, but as educators. The embrace of the educator's stance was "completely obvious" for them, as was the desire "to say with the architecture that this [library] building is not about stuff; it's about people." To foster this view, one needs "librarians who think differently. And I'm afraid I haven't seen a lot of those. I hear a lot of librarians being concerned about our relevance in this age. . . . That's a serious concern, but we're not going to answer it by doing the same old things we've always done." Doing something unusual met with little opposition from college faculty or administrators. Indeed, the library director said she "felt really lucky in the whole process that the administration was actually willing to go out on a limb with this building. And they were not only accepting of some different things to do but really eager to do some different things."

The comments of other library directors suggest how unusual the two planning processes just described are. This librarian, at a liberal arts college (Interview 27), observed that

> Facilities are very expensive. It's hard to figure out how to experiment. . . . We're going to be fairly conservative about that. At least in the college library, what you're going to do will be in response to what you think is happening in the curriculum and the way students are going to use information resources in the next five to ten to fifteen years—whatever your planning horizon is. That's about as far as you're going to go. Those changes in curriculum and so forth are fairly conservative, fairly slow to happen."

The library director at still another liberal arts college (Interview 26) expanded the point, arguing that the general environment of higher education has a conservative influence on library planning: "There doesn't seem to have been a paradigm shift yet [in library space design]. It seems to me that higher education in general does not seem to have paradigm shifts very often. So since other things change so slowly, it may be only natural that libraries do."

This picture of library planning outcomes during the 1990s is mixed, though perhaps less mixed than one would wish. Most of the library directors interviewed for this study, whose experience with projects gave them a well-informed basis for judgment, affirmed largely traditional goals for their libraries. One can hardly quarrel with those goals, especially as they focused on improved accommodations for the readers who had so often been crowded out of the library by growing collections. There was in the 1990s some experimentation in designing library space for the effective use of information technology, but most library directors felt these efforts only qualified but did not fundamentally change the traditional character of library planning and the outcomes of that planning. Efforts to interpolate a quite different vision of the future of libraries into space planning were apparently rare—though successful in the two cases identified in this study.[33]

---

[33] A few library directors spoke of a flexible use of space purposefully designed into their projects as enabling them to make significant changes in the future. In effect, such flexibility becomes an alternative to interpolative planning as a means for guarding today's large capital investments in space from becoming obsolete. This point was made by a library director at a doctoral university (Interview 12), describing a project completed in 1997: "Ultimately, the thing that has saved us is just the opportunity to be flexible and to change with the needs of time. Probably the most outstanding thing I can say about our project [otherwise described as 'pretty traditional'] is that it has given us the opportunity to be completely flexible and grow with the needs of students."

6. Choice of Architect

This study did not collect data on the way architects themselves might influence the extrapolative or interpolative character of library space planning or the outcomes of such planning. Passing comments made by library directors and academic officers indicated high levels of satisfaction with architects. Survey and interview comments warmly praised architects who were attentive to client wishes, suggesting that few architectural firms attempted to reshape the character of space planning where a client was predisposed toward a given planning stance.

Architects are often, but not always, closely associated with the early stages of planning. Libraries are sometimes part of a campus-wide planning effort typically conducted by specialist architects; libraries may also sometimes benefit from campus-wide surveys of building conditions or from a survey focused on the existing library building. The point at which architects most frequently become involved with the academic and other goals of a particular library project is during the actual programming of the project, the stage at which programmatic and adjacency needs get their first conceptual statement, before any design work is undertaken. Early engagement with the architect in developing a deeply shared understanding of the project is critically important to a good match between goals and design decisions; it is equally important in avoiding costly false starts in design and still more costly change orders after construction begins.

This study identified the lead architects for most of the library projects completed in the 1990s. As Figure 7 indicates, architects were known for 388 of the 438 projects (89%) identified in this study. There were 279 different lead architects or architectural firms associated with these 388 projects; architectural firms collaborated on a number of projects, but lead architects only are tabulated here.

FIGURE 7: DISTRIBUTION OF ARCHITECTS
Source: *CLIR Survey* (Table 5)

	Number	% of Total
Projects		
With an architect doing 1 library project only	256	66%
With an architect doing 2 or more library projects	132	34%
Total	*388*	*100%*
Architects		
Doing 1 library project only	256	86%
Doing 2 library projects	28	9%
Doing 3 library projects	8	3%
Doing 4 or more library projects	5	2%
Total	*297*	*100%*

It is striking that 66% of the projects were done by architects who had no other library projects in the study's database, with such architects accounting for 86% of the firms commissioned to build or renovate libraries. Library planning in the 1990s clearly had the benefit of a great variety of professional experience. These figures do not suggest that the selection of architects would itself produce any monotony of thinking about library planning or design.

Just as striking is the evidence of how narrowly focused among architects is substantial experience with libraries. Only 5 firms, among 297, were the lead architects for four or more projects completed in the 1990s.[34] These 5 firms took the lead with 52 projects (some 13% of all projects in the database). If experience matters in library planning and design, as it does in other professional activities, then relatively few projects in the 1990s had the benefit of lead architects with substantial experience. Such experience is doubtless a competitive advantage from the architects' point of view. From the point of view of the vast majority of institutions that are unlikely to secure this degree of experience in their library architects, it would be important to find ways to learn as much as possible from the example of architects having wide experience with libraries. The responsibility for identifying and acting on opportunities for such learning lies, surely, with the library profession itself.[35]

7. Ownership of the Planning Process

The chief academic officers and other principal administrators interviewed for this study identified an important and distinctive characteristic of library space planning. Unlike other academic buildings, faculty do not assert an owner's right to control library planning. This opens the door for others to own the planning process. The dean at a liberal arts college (Interview 6) explained the matter as follows:

> The library planning is almost more like the campus center planning we had. . . . It's a common space; it's not anyone's

---

[34] These were, in alphabetical order, Davis, Brody and Associates (New York); Hillier (Princeton); Perry Dean Rogers (Boston); Shepley Bulfinch Richardson and Abbott (Boston); and Woollen Molzan and Partners (Indianapolis). The vice president at a doctoral university (Interview 3) commented on the way a few architectural firms have come to occupy prominent specialist positions in library design. Speaking of one such company, this officer said he hopes the firm "has it right." His comment did not express skepticism so much as a recognition of the inherent risks involved in so many colleges and universities depending on the expertise of the firm in a fast-changing environment where there are few means for validating the firm's judgments.

[35] Efforts along this line are evident in a number of publications. See, for instance, Karen Commings, "Inside the University of Southern California's 'Cybrary,'" *Computers in Libraries* 14 (November/December 1994), 18–19; see also, Webb 2000, Crosbie and Hickey 2001, and Jones 1999. The Crosbie and Hickey volume includes a useful commentary by Hickey (pp. 8–18) in which he identifies nine factors that powerfully influenced the design of the libraries reviewed in his book: (1) the growing importance of electronics, (2) the shift from exclusively individual learning to individual-and-collective learning, (3) community and institutional pride, (4) the emerging role of libraries as campus centers and information commons, (5) the need for less expensive ways to shelve printed materials, (6) the importance of historical materials and special collections, (7) differing concepts about staff-staff and staff-user relationships, (8) uncertainty about the future, and (9) site, budget, and design considerations. In additional to publications, there is a good deal of attention paid to space planning in librarians' professional meetings and symposia. See, for instance, the Third Annual ARL/OCLC Institute Strategic Issues Forum, "Future Library Architecture: Conception, Design, and Use of Library Space," February 15–17, 2002, at http://www.oclc.org/institute/events/lv/Future_Library_Architecture_ Draft_Agenda.pdf. See also the programmatic activities of two groups within the Library Administration and Management Association, the BES Buildings for College and University Libraries, and the BES Libraries Facilities Planning Discussion Group at http://www.ala.org/Content/NavigationMenu/Our_ Association/Divisions/LAMA/LAMA.htm.

space in particular. And so as a result, people such as myself have more of an opportunity to make an impact than in . . . [academic buildings in the sciences and arts], where it [i.e., the new building] is . . . sort of owned by the faculty members in that particular discipline.

Many library directors would say that, on the contrary, virtually everyone asserts owner's rights to influence planning, so that building or renovating a library necessarily involves a complex and normally prolonged process of negotiation.

Of course, academic buildings always require negotiated decisions about priorities, project budgets, sites, and, often, exterior appearances. Decisions on these matters are seen to affect many campus interests and must for that reason be made as institutional decisions. But beyond these matters, the occupants of a building normally claim an owner's right to have their views deferred to on anything that will determine the building's success in meeting its academic goals. What do the interviews conducted for this study indicate about the assertion and management of ownership roles in library space planning?

Chief academic officers not surprisingly focus first on their financial responsibility for library planning projects. Such responsibilities normally include enabling decisions that set the project's priority among competing claims on capital resources and ensure funding for the project.[36] These decisions are sometimes made in the context of larger plans for campus-wide renovation. On occasion, project decisions are part of a disappointing history of false starts. One president (Interview 5) spoke particularly of his responsibility to overcome a long history of being rebuffed by the state for capital funds for the library. Academic officers commonly avoid detailed involvement in a project. The executive vice president of a doctoral university, for instance, described himself as "an enabler of sensible academic plans. I tend not to get involved in the details, but I feel empowered to reject them out of hand if they're silly" (Interview 3). Academic officers rarely asserted other roles in the interviews, even when they played them. Where the library director at a doctoral university described his chief academic officer as the "godfather" and "guardian angel" of the project, that officer himself (Interview 1) confined his role to that of appointing a good planning group. The creativity of the planning was, he said, "very much grass-roots driven. It came from some really creative faculty and some very creative deans, and my particular role at that point was to make sure they had the money and to get out of their way." He did, however, strongly encourage the planning group "to push to the limits, to take some risks." Generally, library directors and academic officers agreed on the vital but limited roles of the latter in library planning. The library directors interviewed for

---

[36] The library director at a liberal arts college described the impact of a newly appointed president, who had made facilities and space planning his primary agenda and approved a more aggressive approach to library renovations. Responding to a preliminary planning document, the president sent the library director an e-mail message saying that the project "will probably cost twice as much, and let's go ahead and do it. When I got that, I said, 'Hmm, I don't think I've ever received an e-mail like that before.'"

this study, who had all completed projects, spoke of having invaluable support from institutional officers, but very few described those officers as taking any ownership role beyond that of a broadly defined financial responsibility for the project.

Few library projects are planned without the involvement of both faculty and students as members either of a standing library advisory committee or of a specially appointed space planning committee. In this way, they have opportunities for a detailed involvement in planning—and for project ownership—that academic officers generally disavow. Faculty and students typically do not, however, act on these opportunities.

The faculty roles that emerged most strongly in the interviews were those of vetoing bad ideas and of approving, but not generating, good ones. The dean of the liberal arts college quoted above (Interview 6) made the first of these roles clear in explaining what he meant in describing faculty participation in planning as "strong." He said that faculty worked in a collegial way with the architect, librarians, and administration. The most critical juncture came with a potentially controversial decision to treat one floor as a basement for shelving. Faculty "flexibility" in accepting this decision was critically important to keeping the library project within budget. The power to veto key decisions described here was also explicitly identified by the library director at a doctoral university (Interview 7), where again a key decision involved shelving. Library staff addressed faculty misgivings about using available space for purposes other than shelving through individual conversations and through the conversion to project goals of an influential historian, who became convinced of the value of what the librarians were proposing instead of shelving and appreciated the library's efforts to develop online resources for history. Teaching faculty, this librarian said, "can block [a project] if they want to. . . . I learned about campus politics." Both this librarian and the college dean emphasized the value of avoiding conflicts that would likely find expression in faculty vetoes.

Asked whether faculty members played a more creative role in library space planning, the college dean just quoted (Interview 6) described faculty as reactive rather than proactive. "They were not on our committee what I would characterize as being the generator of ideas." The dean went on to say that

> the question is how much real investment do faculty have? And they're invested in the library, but it's not like where they live. . . . [Unlike the library, other academic buildings are] where these people live and work every day. So their involvement with respect to making suggestions and pushing various things [in these other buildings] is really noticeable. It's a huge difference. . . . With the library, I had the feeling that people don't feel as personally invested. . . . They want to have a good library, they want to make sure that we can continue to develop the collection and that students will have a good place to work, . . . but I don't see the faculty feeling like it's some place they're going to spend most of their working hours. And so I don't see them

as having that kind or level of involvement with the project. If I look at where most of the ideas came from, they came from the architects, the library staff, or the administrators such as myself and the president. The faculty were involved, and we wanted to make sure that it would work well for the faculty, but I can't say that they were the engines behind the planning.

A responding, non-ownership involvement by faculty in planning was evident in another project, at a liberal arts college, where the faculty library committee served primarily as a sounding board for the project and to build faculty ownership of it. The committee readily signed off on the educational features of the project and spent much of its time deliberating on less critical issues, such as carpet color (Interview 29). Such characterizations of faculty involvement typify much of what was said in the other interviews and in many survey comments. Faculty, it appears, commonly assert more of a judge's role than an owner's role in library planning.

Students, who benefited so dramatically from many of the library projects of the 1990s, had the least ownership-like role in planning. Library directors repeatedly commented on the difficulty of sustaining student engagement in planning. The most obvious difficulty was continuing student membership in planning committee work that might extend over several years. It was, however, often possible to get invaluable feedback from students on quite specific questions, such as the choice of seating and the provision of group study spaces. The experience at one doctoral university was particularly dramatic, with student participation starting strong but then dissipating. Before renovations, the library director reported (Interview 12), students were "overall appalled [with the library]. In general, the student view of things was 'Don't go there; you won't find anything you need.' We were just sort of a place that did not figure in students' lives." This indifference was matched by an indisposition on the part of campus administrators and the state legislature to act on library needs. But a new provost arrived and students organized a sit-in to complain about the library. Student activism caught the attention of the president, who commissioned a consultant's report. As the project gathered support, the student senate authorized a referendum, passed overwhelmingly, which allocated student fee money to the library project. For all this activism and commitment, student desires for the project were, according to the library director, "relatively visceral." They included air conditioning, a study space open 24 hours a day, access to food and drink, and group study space. Even in this unusual case, student involvement in library space planning came to be primarily that of a consumer. The evidence of both the study survey and the interviews indicates that students identify themselves as consumers and are treated—with respect, it should be said—as consumers by others involved in library planning.

Who then owns library space planning? Most often it is library staff and especially the library director, working with the architect and the institution's facilities staff. Such arrangements are entirely consistent with the deference usually paid in higher education to the judgment of a building's occupants. On operational matters—ranging from reference and circulation services to technical services and to the security and environmental conditions needed to protect collections—the professional judgment of librarians is properly respected and normally prevails within bounds set by the project budget.[37] In considering how library space might best facilitate student learning and faculty teaching, topics not squarely within librarians' professional competence in the way that library operations are, the evidence is clear that librarians rarely undertake systematic assessments or seek substantive guidance from students and faculty themselves. One library director after another described, instead, their reliance on direct observation of the behaviors of readers and the liaison structures often built with individual academic programs. The special project manager at one liberal arts college (Interview 28) described this planning strategy and the library's confidence in it:

> We didn't do formal surveys. Given the size of [the college] . . . there's an awful lot of comfortable interaction—library with students, library with faculty, several librarians are on the faculty council. [There has been] on campus . . . a very comfortable respect by faculty and students for the library. I think we felt the communication routes were in place, that a formal survey wouldn't be the best way to hear what people wanted. All along there's very active involvement with and keeping up with not only what the curriculum is now but where it's going. I think there's a very good sense of where the faculty wants to go as well as how students are doing their work. So it made more sense to us not to be formal but to take advantage of the communication routes that we had.[38]

Staff responsible for the design of an electronic classroom at a master's degree institution reported (Interview 23) no student involvement in planning for the classroom. Planners depended on their own teaching experience for their understanding of how students learn. The library director at a liberal arts college (Interview 26) reported that 80% of the design decisions were made by library and other involved staff, drawing on their own observation of faculty teaching practices. The college is small enough so that these academic support staff members understand campus teaching methods and needs quite well. The library director did not claim an equally strong parallel knowledge of student learning behaviors. The library director at another master's degree institution reported that neither he nor his staff had had any previous experience in building new

---

[37] Deference to the good professional judgment of librarians was evident in the actions of the chief academic officer at a master's degree institution, whose chief contribution according to the library director (Interview 22) was to tell people to "leave the library alone" as it planned and built the new facility.

[38] This librarian reported the involvement of students in planning "was primarily [through] those who worked for us. You might say they were biased. And of course they are. But they can also speak with us with some understanding of what we can possibly do for them. And some of the most valuable information I got was from our student employees. And the thing I remember most was what kind of furniture they want. . . ."

libraries and were nervous about the task. Working with an attentive architect was helpful:

> Afterward . . . we felt fairly confident that we had zeroed in on what the campus needed, basically. I did not feel as guilty about not doing formal studies and having the time to come up with a plan that was based on surveys and years of thought. . . . Some of this was instinct and our years in the profession—what we had observed. Trying to tap into that and hoping that was accurate. Not a very good thing to say you relied on, when you're spending a lot of money, especially taxpayers' money. We had a confidence level that sustained us throughout. . . . I think getting a consultant in here helped us shape this thing.

It would be unfair to say that the conceptual ownership of library space planning falls to librarians by default. Their professional expertise in managing service operations and their observation of reader behaviors go far toward justifying the deference in planning decisions that project owners rightly claim. But it can be said that lodging ownership with librarians is likely to ensure that planning will give first priority to the operational needs of libraries. Other needs, especially those of students, tend to get less systematic assessment and less well-considered response. Such needs would be better served by a more imaginative, collaborative fixing of ownership responsibility for planning.

The consequences of the somewhat fractured ownership of planning described here occasionally appeared in study data in the form of plans that missed, or nearly missed, important changes in the culture of learning and teaching or that achieved striking success as much because of good fortune as because of informed planning. The case of one library that failed initially to understand the need of students to work in pairs or larger groups at workstations has already been cited. The library director at another doctoral university (Interview 7) described how her renovation plans originally included only a large room for computing. During construction itself, it became clear that what was needed was the ability to distribute electronic resources. So library plans were changed to emphasize networking. "These changes were almost forced by the teaching side," she said, through changes in instruction that involved an increasing use of electronic resources and the university's course-support software.

The language of chance figured importantly in a few interviews. The library director at a doctoral institution (Interview 12) has already been quoted as saying of an immensely popular group study space that "we somehow stumbled into a really high-use kind of thing here" and that "somehow it just all came together as a very useful space for students." More tellingly, the president at another doctoral university (Interview 5) had made the library his signature project, motivated by "an incredible need . . . to just simply have a place to keep the materials. That drove everything in my mind. Secondly was this notion of an electronic access point." When asked about reader accommodations, this president described how little students had used the former library. "The academic tenor of the institution was being negatively influenced by just simply the cramped physical conditions." The library director and especially one dean on the advisory committee made it their business to build excellent reader accommodations into the project. "That has worked out brilliantly. You go to the library now, and it is a very active and alive place, and I think that may be the singularly most important outcome of our project." Asked if he intended this going into the project, the president said, "No. My most important outcomes were finding a place to put the books and secondly trying, again, to make sure that the library was the information center of the campus, both in terms of hard materials and access to the external media." This president described the success of reader accommodations as "some form of serendipity, I guess," at least as regards his intentions for a project to which he had committed himself so strongly.

8. Partnerships in Planning Library Space for an Impact on Learning

This essay does not argue that academic libraries were poorly planned in the 1990s or that the outcomes of that planning failed to serve readers well. There is abundant evidence of the success of the library projects studied here, not least the evidence of heavy student use of library space that had been thoughtfully designed for them. This essay does however argue that library planning in the 1990s was not systematically informed about modes of student learning and faculty teaching, precisely the arenas in which academic library space could have its "singularly most important outcome" as regards the fundamental mission of college and universities.

The difference between the information commons, a feature of libraries that became popular in the 1990s, and a hypothetical learning commons suggests how limited was the engagement of planners with self-directed learning behaviors among students. These two terms—*information commons* and *learning commons*—draw upon the long heritage of common rooms in higher education, where all members of the academic community can meet informally around shared interests, especially after meals. There are, however, important differences between the two terms.

Information commons emphasize the interdisciplinary character of information and the power of digital technology to manage apparently disparate information resources as one. In effect, information commons marry the best offerings of information technology staff and of librarians. Such spaces characteristically provide readers with highly capable computers offering a wide variety of information management software and access to the richest possible set of information resources. Information commons also provide to readers staff with expertise in information resources and technology who offer both one-on-one and group instruction on how best to exploit the resources of the information commons. Readers are invited to explore, experiment, and learn information management skills useful to them as students and teachers and, indeed, as lifelong learners. Information commons respond imaginatively to the need to help readers master information technology as electronic information resources proliferated and the tasks of judging their value and employing them skillfully became strikingly more complex.[39] If one were looking for analog campus spaces, one would think of language laboratories. Both are designed and managed by specialists to achieve specific pedagogical goals. Both create resource-rich environments with specialist staff helping students learn particular skills essential to a liberal education.

A learning commons, as imagined here, would have quite different goals. It would bring people together not around informally shared interests, as happens in traditional common rooms, but around shared learning tasks, sometimes formalized in class assignments. The core activity of a learning commons would not be the manipulation and mastery of information, as in an information commons, but the collaborative learning by which students turn information into knowledge and sometimes into wisdom. A learning commons would be built around the social dimensions of learning and knowledge and would be managed by students themselves for learning purposes that vary greatly and change frequently. The undergraduate dean at a doctoral university (Interview 2) emphasized the need, in designing library space, to

> change the point of view from, 'Here are the [library] services I want to offer to you, therefore I'm going to array myself this way,' to 'What are the processes and functions that students and faculty engaged in inquiry would be looking to do,' and . . . shift . . . [the] vantage point so that we would organize things that made sense from a functional processing standpoint—have that be a guiding principle. Also recognizing that . . . [the requirements for learning-based design are] very fluid. . . . The rate of change of those [learning functions] is very high. So we have to be able to be adaptive and flexible. And I think we've envisioned that there would be ways to reconfigure space.

The library director (Interview 8) at the doctoral university described in section 5 of this essay as aiming at a fundamentally different kind of library spoke of the difficulty of designing highly adaptive space. On the one hand, it "is quite amazing how, without having any particular prompting, students have always felt comfortable gathering chairs and using white boards and things" in the library. Nonetheless, this librarian reported

> the designers had wanted it to be even much more dramatic than I think it was in reality. There was a lot of talk about just open space—leave furniture so students can rearrange it in ways that suit their needs. Projects could happen in that space and then go away—almost like an academic playground of sorts. . . . They very much had thought of something that would allow students

---

[39] For a further account of the information commons, see Donald Beagle, "Conceptualizing an Information Commons," *Journal of Academic Librarianship* 25 (1999), 82–89.

to be very hands-on. I don't think in practice they could figure
out how really to make that work though.

The greatest challenge in designing a learning commons is to
conceive of it as "owned" by learners, not by teachers, whether faculty or librarians. A learning commons must accommodate frequently
changing learning tasks that students define them for themselves,
not information-management tasks defined and taught by library or
academic computing staff. A learning commons would most likely
also provide some kind of food service, maintaining the strong cus-
tomary association between food and socially shaped activities.

While the dean and library director just quoted both imagined
something like a learning commons as a library facility, such space
might conceivably be located elsewhere—in, for instance, a student
center. The immense advantage of a library location is that only there
can the learning commons be surrounded by a rich, comprehensive
environment of print, electronic, and human information resources.
Because the function of a learning commons is to enable students to
manage their own learning, it must for that reason be designed both
to prompt and facilitate the use of the full range of library resources
that colleges and universities assemble to support learning. In this
way, the learning commons, as imagined here, becomes perhaps the
single most powerful spatial expression of the educational role of
the library. Such library space has value not simply because it ac-
commodates the use of information but more particularly because it
embeds that use in the fundamental learning activities, pursued collaboratively, that define the mission of colleges and universities and
to which information use is always secondary.

Looking for models of the learning commons, one finds elements
of it in dining halls and residential common rooms, in library reading
rooms, in the collaborative ethos of scientific laboratories and "think
tank" buildings, and in some bookstores. This study found no library
project using the term *learning commons*. It found many projects that
succeed in providing students with an inviting set of reading and
collaborative study spaces, although none of them were designed
with the benefit of a well-informed understanding of students' most
successful modes of learning.

It is possible to imagine a planning process that does not forgo
what was so successful in the projects of the 1990s but that begins
to exploit more systematically the educational potential of library
space. Achieving this potential will require not only "librarians who
think differently," but also a planning process with at least two unusual characteristics:

- First, library design should not be dominated primarily by a
  concern for information resources and their delivery—by, for instance, such facilities as information commons that emphasize delivery systems and hardware likely to change rapidly and become
  increasingly less dependent on bricks-and-mortar space. Library
  design should incorporate a deeper understanding of the independent, active learning behaviors of students and the teaching strategies of faculty meant to support those behaviors. Such design

could create libraries where, in the words quoted at the beginning of this essay, learning "happens" as well as places where learning is "supported."

- Second, our understanding of the library as education space—as, for instance, a learning commons—will be only weakly and inconsistently advanced if librarians engage with students primarily as consumers of library services and with faculty principally as power brokers in campus politics. Students and faculty do indeed play these roles, which must be respected. But meaningful engagement with their substantive activities as learners and teachers should not be conceived primarily as a negotiation that sustains and ultimately ratifies the librarian's ownership of the planning process. Instead, that engagement should aim at a genuine planning partnership with faculty and students shaped around substantive questions and not the management of differences in power and status. This partnership should construct a shared understanding throughout the campus community of key issues in learning and teaching and their implication for library space. One sees relatively few examples of such partnerships between librarians and faculty. But they exist—in, for instance, some bibliographic instruction programs and in some centers for teaching and learning—and they can be nurtured.[40] Such partnerships will necessarily be at the heart of any effort to design library buildings that are primarily about people as learners, rather than about the information "stuff" that supports learning.

This study found much evidence that librarians attentively observe campus teaching and learning behaviors, but very few examples of anything beyond observation that might approximate a genuine planning partnership. The library director at a doctoral university (Interview 10) reported an admirably sustained engagement with students. He has established a standing student advisory board and a student liaison position. The latter is a paid hourly position (now also earning tuition remission) functioning as a kind of ombudsman. Students apply for this position. The liaison position is also involved in arranging programmatic activities attracting a student audience and in strategic planning for the library. The position has "been very, very successful." It has a board and open meetings, with agendas, that students are invited to attend:

> We listen to them [i.e., students] as they tell us what they like and don't like about the library. . . . We get their input on budget issues. When we go to our advisory board, we lay out a whole series of things and talk with them about what they sense the priorities are. And that has really been very helpful. We have learned so much about what the students are thinking that it has helped us tremendously.

---

[40] For an account of the strong partnership effort among librarians, faculty, and information technology staff in planning the pioneering Leavey Library at the University of Southern California as a teaching library, see Holmes-Wong, Afifi, and Bahavar 1997.

Otherwise, this study found little evidence that library space planning in the 1990s attempted systematically to understand modes of student learning or the possible impact of learning behaviors on library space design. And aside from some nascent involvement with campus centers for teaching and learning, this study found no evidence of library space planning being informed by a systematic understanding of faculty teaching or by assessments of how library space might be designed to advance faculty efforts to shape the campus teaching environment, both inside and outside of the classroom.

Would systematically built and applied knowledge of the modes of student learning and faculty teaching produce appreciably different results in library design? Would such knowledge lead to anything different from the electronic classrooms and group study spaces that over the last decade have become common features of library plans? It is impossible to answer these questions with confidence in the absence of some experience of planning efforts strongly informed by a substantive knowledge of student learning and faculty teaching behaviors. This essay argues, however, that library space planning will not advance much beyond existing practice as long as it engages with students primarily as consumers and with faculty primarily as holders of veto power. The evidence of this study indicates that such planning stances produce, at their worst, little more than agreement on carpet colors. At their best, they get to decisions about furniture. Such decisions can in fact be quite important, as it is possibly the case that given the importance of flexibility in the use of space, "what makes a building a library is a set of medium- to small-scale decisions which principally involve furniture."[41] Extracting the greatest possible educational benefit from furniture decisions is clearly a central concern of electronic classroom design.[42] But otherwise decisions about library furniture—the furniture that does so much to define and shape our experience of libraries—has little to do with learning and much to do with comfort and durability. These traditional concerns are surely important, but they may blinker planners to ways in which furniture could be designed and deployed to enhance the educational impact of investments in library space.

There are numerous people who manage learning spaces from whom library designers might learn regarding both furniture and larger-scale issues in how people shape learning environments. They include, for instance "think tank" managers, laboratory scientists, and student services staff. Such people are, however, rarely consulted. In explaining this failure to explore wider thinking and to gain the benefit of alternative experience, the director at a large branch library serving a doctoral university (Interview 9) commented:

> In some ways it would be nice to think of the library in the larger
> context at the university level and think what other services
> would be appropriate for the library [building] and to build those

---

41 See Michael Brawne, "Interiors in Detail," p.216 in *Library Builders,* 1997.

42 See, for instance, Lisa Janicke Hinchliffe, *Neal-Schuman Electronic Classroom Handbook* (New York: Neal-Schuman, 2001).

things into the library. Sometimes I think those discussions don't always take place, and I think they should. What happens within the library world is that you worry you're going to lose your space. It becomes 'your space,' and you're giving it up for some other function instead of thinking, well, what are the services and programs we'd like to put in this central campus building, and how do we design them cohesively?

Asked whether she saw any opportunities for significant change in library space planning—for an interpolative approach to such planning that would include thinking that is now largely excluded—this library director replied:

> If I had a blank piece of paper and the promise of some funds to be able to do something different, the first thing I would do is work with the office of student services, the . . . technology folks, and say, 'What are the services we want in this building? And how do we achieve some synergy among our programs to be able to provide that?' That would be my starting point, and I think that is perhaps revolutionary in that libraries haven't shared their space necessarily with other campus entities. Or their thinking.

The value of a wide sharing of thinking is suggested by the library director at another doctoral university (Interview 13), who has invested an extraordinary effort in the preliminary, goal-defining stage of planning. He described the process as beginning with a campus-wide committee of faculty, graduate and undergraduate students, information technology staff, and librarians appointed by the provost and charged to re-vision the library. The committee worked for 18 months, "putting a stake in the ground about what this place should look like." Its report was widely reviewed and commented on throughout the campus. An architect was hired only after this process was completed. One of the things that strongly emerged in the report was the rich set of opportunities the library has for collaboration. These opportunities spring fundamentally from a new undergraduate curriculum the university is putting in place, featuring new requirements for writing and research that have library implications. The College of Arts and Sciences has established a center for teaching, learning, and writing to offer tutorial assistance to students. The center has a satellite operation in the library. That drives the need for group study space, not otherwise adequately provided elsewhere on campus. The new curriculum also includes some information technology competencies. The library needs to create "spaces where that can happen."

The vice president at this institution (Interview 3) commended the library director as "really dedicated to having a campus-wide consultation." In describing the success of this consultative process, the vice president remarked on the length of time it took. When asked whether a process already so lengthy and collaborative would benefit from a substantive exploration of learning modes and teaching methods, he replied in the negative. He felt that at his highly selective institution, good learning happens for reasons intrinsic to the institution. He suspects that less selective schools might want to pay close attention in space design to successful student learning behaviors, but at his university such inquiries would produce improvements only on the margin. "I don't think we spend a lot of time thinking about marginal improvements in pedagogy, or things like that. We sort of take for granted that smart kids learn things. . . . When you look at the quality of the whole experience, that wouldn't be a place where I would spend a lot of time." The dean of the undergraduate college and the library director at this institution, by contrast, affirmed the importance of modeling the implications for library space planning of what we know about the most successful modes of student learning.[43]

The argument of this study is that at colleges and universities where good learning is not somehow "intrinsic" to the institution, and even at those where it is but where there is some wish to understand why the institution's environment is so successful, systematic attention to students' most successful learning modes and to faculty teaching behaviors should be an explicit part of library space planning. It is true that this study cannot document the value of such attention, given that it discovered no instances of it. We simply do not know what we do not—yet—know. But it is hard to see other means by which academic library space can be brought so strongly into line with an institution's fundamental learning and teaching missions. And surely it makes little sense for the higher education community to continue to invest massively in library space without exploring every possible benefit of that investment.

It is clear that in the 1990s, the single most powerful motivator of library construction and renovation was the traditional need to provide shelving for growing collections. Remarkably, however, few of the library directors and academic officers who guided projects in the 1990s expect future projects to be motivated so strongly by shelving needs. The shift in thinking (if not yet in a large number of project outcomes) documented in this study should be seen as an opportunity for interpolative planning rooted in the educational function of libraries.[44] Such planning will start with an affirmation that library buildings are primarily and inviolably about people, not about "stuff." This affirmation should not be seen as slighting the function of the library to provide access to information; it only recognizes that such provision will increasingly be met in the virtual space

[43] This library director knows, however, how different his view is from that prevailing on campus. No formal assessment of student learning modes was undertaken as part of the library's re-visioning study. This omission resulted in part from "a level of [faculty] complacency about thinking we know how students learn. . . . We run up against it all the time with the instructional technology piece of what we're doing. The new curriculum forced everyone to rethink what they were doing in the classroom. . . . There were certain kinds of requirements in terms of research and other competencies that we're trying to develop within the curriculum . . . . For some faculty, this was incredibly threatening because it was seen as a challenge to what they were traditionally doing in the classroom."

[44] For the views of one library architect along such lines, see Geoffrey T. Freeman, "The Academic Library in the 21st Century: Partner in Education," pp. 168–175 in Webb 2000.

created by the library's electronic systems, while its building has other primary functions. Projects completed in the 1990s evince some understanding of this fundamental shift in the functions of library buildings, and these projects achieved some success in acting on this new understanding. These accomplishments found memorable expression in the pride and pleasure of the library director, quoted earlier (Interview 12), who described regularly finding his library always full of students:

> literally every chair, . . . and they're all talking at the same time. And the hum that rises above this is just amazing. And they don't care. . . . There's all this din that occurs [from] hundreds of students in this same space, all working together and all talking at the same time. . . . Somehow it just all came together as a very useful space for students. . . . We just beam with pride. Every time I come down the elevator to leave, and I see these hundreds of students out there—that just never happened before.

The responsibility to inform library space planning with a systematically developed knowledge of how students learn and faculty teach lies before the academic community. It is a responsibility for all who care deeply about libraries, who must learn to work in campus-wide partnership to make library buildings fit homes for the social dimension of the learning and teaching process by which knowledge moves between people and its embodiment in printed books and in fleeting electronic digits. Happily, the fresh vision and interpolative planning that will be required to produce such results will be the most fitting, and at the same time the most powerful, way to perpetuate the traditional impulse to make library space celebratory space—to design an *esprit de place* into libraries.[45]

---

[45] See Demas and Scherer 2002.

PART 2:
DATA TABLES AND CHARTS

This section contains a report of the study data. The intention is to enable readers to appraise these data independently of the interpretative essay in part 1.

The data consist of (1) the quantitative data from the study survey, (2) a summary of the qualitative comments made by survey respondents, (3) summaries and partial transcriptions of telephone interviews with library directors and academic officers, and (4) the quantitative data from an independent survey, conducted in 2001 for the Council of Independent Colleges (CIC), on matters closely related to the concerns of this study. As explained below, some particularly large data sets are not reproduced here but are readily available in the online version of this report, available at http://www.clir.org/pubs/abstract/pub122abst.html.

The quantitative data are presented in tabular and graph forms, along with brief explanations of how to read the tables. See part 3 of this report for an account of the research methodologies used in gathering and analyzing the study data.

Quantitative Data from the Study Survey

Table 1 reports, by year from 1992 through 2001, much of the data available in the list of capital projects at academic libraries published annually in the December issue of *Library Journal* (*LJ*). The data are drawn directly from *LJ* and are self-explanatory. The table also provides (1) a column reporting the real dollar value of projects, (2) statistical measures of the annual variability of several factors, and (3) statistical summaries of most columns for the decade covered by the study.

TABLE 1. *Library Journal* **building statistics**

Reporting Year		Total # Projects	z score for total projects	Total Current Dollar Project Cost (x $1 million)	GDP Deflator Index (2001 = 1.000)	Total Real Dollar Project Cost in 2001 Dollars (x $1 million)	z score for total real dollar costs	Total Gross Square Feet	z score for total gross square feet	Total Book Capacity (x 1,000)	z score for total book capacity	Total Gross Square Feet of New Buildings only	New GSF as a % of Total GSF	z score for % of new GSF	Book Capacity (x 1,000) in New GSF
1992					0.6267										
	New buildings	18		162.776		259.735		1,379,713		5,859		1,379,713	33.4%	-0.71	
	Additions and renovations	21		175.956		280.766		2,252,220		13,573					
	Additions only	4		42.742		68.202		385,175		2,825					
	Renovations only	6		103.949		165.867		119,208		2,191					
	Subtotals	*49*	*1.37*	*485.423*		*774.570*	*2.04*	*4,136,316*	*1.55*	*24,448*	*1.90*				
1993					0.6588										
	New buildings	21		227.169		344.822		1,638,409		6,804		1,638,409	42.2%	0.27	
	Additions and renovations	14		121.496		184.420		1,459,491		6,843					
	Additions only	4		49.313		74.853		296,000		2,175					
	Renovations only	12		41.153		62.467		489,432		2,707					
	Subtotals	*51*	*1.62*	*439.131*		*666.562*	*1.37*	*3,883,332*	*1.24*	*18,529*	*0.77*				
1994					0.6997										
	New buildings	17		191.919		274.288		1,558,133		5,588		1,558,133	53.9%	1.57	
	Additions and renovations	8		83.438		119.248		955,878		6,398					
	Additions only	5		55.719		79.633		197,070		740					
	Renovations only	8		8.817		12.601		180,491		651					
	Subtotals	*38*	*0.01*	*339.893*		*485.770*	*0.23*	*2,891,572*	*0.02*	*13,377*	*-0.22*				
1995					0.7340										
	New buildings	9		69.757		95.037		521,024		2,815		521,024	24.7%	-1.67	
	Additions and renovations	11		89.183		121.503		1,021,351		4,454					
	Additions only	0		0.000		0.000		0		0					
	Renovations only	6		78.954		107.567		571,102		2,406					
	Subtotals	*26*	*-1.47*	*237.894*		*324.106*	*-0.79*	*2,113,477*	*-0.93*	*9,675*	*-0.92*				
1996					0.7749										
	New buildings	18		181.451		234.161		1,477,652		4,346		1,477,652	45.4%	0.63	
	Additions and renovations	13		142.477		183.865		1,624,290		7,359					
	Additions only	0		0.000		0.000		0		0					
	Renovations only	9		17.128		22.103		153,206		1,071					
	Subtotals	*40*	*0.26*	*341.056*		*440.129*	*-0.06*	*3,255,148*	*0.47*	*12,776*	*-0.33*				
1997					0.8251										
	New buildings	14		181.166		219.569		1,055,948		3,331		1,055,948	37.4%	-0.26	
	Additions and renovations	16		112.924		136.861		1,508,271		6,748					
	Additions only	0		0.000		0.000		0		0					
	Renovations only	8		18.748		22.722		258,568		678					
	Subtotals	*38*	*0.01*	*312.838*		*379.152*	*-0.44*	*2,822,787*	*-0.06*	*10,757*	*-0.72*				
1998					0.8710										
	New buildings	17		234.684		269.442		1,255,930		6,651		1,255,930	39.8%	0.01	
	Additions and renovations	13		128.700		147.761		1,623,845		6,316					
	Additions only	0		0.000		0.000		0		0					
	Renovations only	5		5.548		6.370		276,999		3,532					
	Subtotals	*35*	*-0.36*	*368.932*		*423.573*	*-0.16*	*3,156,774*	*0.35*	*16,499*	*0.38*				
1999					0.9199										
	New buildings	11		160.026		173.960		916,098		4,946		916,098	42.8%	0.35	
	Additions and renovations	6		108.391		117.829		995,380		5,355					
	Additions only	2		2.500		2.718		8,500		0					
	Renovations only	11		15.516		16.867		218,349		1,263					
	Subtotals	*30*	*-0.97*	*286.433*		*311.374*	*-0.87*	*2,138,327*	*-0.90*	*11,564*	*-0.56*				
2000					0.9745										
	New buildings	10		180.675		185.403		737,380		4,993		737,380	51.1%	1.26	
	Additions and renovations	6		40.184		41.236		378,043		1,249					
	Additions only	2		25.585		26.254		112,000		135					
	Renovations only	12		17.096		17.543		216,681		1,180					
	Subtotals	*30*	*-0.97*	*263.540*		*270.436*	*-1.13*	*1,444,104*	*-1.75*	*7,557*	*-1.33*				
2001					1.0000										
	New buildings	12		167.167		167.167		768,428		4,145		768,428	26.6%	-1.46	
	Additions and renovations	12		200.108		200.108		1,558,969		13,296					
	Additions only	0		0.000		0.000		0		0					
	Renovations only	18		51.581		51.581		566,354		2,387					
	Subtotals	*42*	*0.51*	*418.856*		*418.856*	*-0.19*	*2,893,751*	*0.02*	*19,828*	*1.02*				
Ten year total		379				4,494.528		28,735,588		145,010		11,308,715			49,478
Mean		37.9				449.453		2,873,559		14,501		1,130,872	39.7%		4,948
Standard deviation		8.1				159.030		816,834		5,227		386,986	9.0%		1,323

TABLE 2. Study survey demographics

Carnegie Classification category	All Institutions		Study Population		Study Sample	
	Frequency	Percent	Frequency	Percent	Frequency	Percent
Doctoral/Research Universities—Extensive	151	3.8%	142	32.1%	77	32.1%
Doctoral/Research Universities—Intensive	110	2.8%	35	7.9%	26	10.8%
Master's Colleges and Universities I	496	12.6%	102	23.0%	55	22.9%
Master's Colleges and Universities II	114	2.9%	13	2.9%	6	2.5%
Baccalaureate Colleges—Liberal Arts	226	5.7%	51	11.5%	29	12.1%
Baccalaureate Colleges—General	324	8.2%	24	5.4%	13	5.4%
Baccalaureate/Associate's Colleges	57	1.4%	5	1.1%	1	0.4%
Associate's Colleges	1,669	42.3%	26	5.9%	13	5.4%
Specialized Institutions	767	19.5%	32	7.2%	17	7.1%
Tribal Colleges and Universities	28	0.7%	1	0.2%	0	0.0%
Unclassified	0	0.0%	12	2.7%	3	1.3%
Total	3,942	100.0%	443	100.0%	240	100.0%

Table 2 shows the number of institutions in the survey's database of capital projects distributed by the institutional classification categories used by the Carnegie Foundation for the Advancement of Education (at http://www.carnegiefoundation.org/Classification/CIHE2000/Tables.htm). The first column lists institution types. The next three pairs of columns report the number of institutions and the percentage of all institutions found in (1) the Carnegie classification scheme, (2) the study database of institutions to which surveys were sent (the study population), and (3) the survey responses (the study sample).

Chart 1 derives from the study sample (i.e., the institutions that responded to the study survey). It reports the distribution by size (i.e., number of gross square feet) of all library projects in the sample.

Chart 2 derives from the study sample (i.e., the institutions that responded to the study survey). It reports the distribution by size (i.e., number of gross square feet) of library projects in the sample that involved 100,000 gross square feet or less.

Table 3a reports the responses to question 1 in the study survey. Question 1 identified several different possible motivators (items a–n in the first column) for library capital projects and asked respondents to indicate on a six-point scale how strongly each factor motivated the respondent's project. The percentage of all responses to a given motivator (e.g., "growth of library staff") that occupied a given point in the response scale (e.g., "not a factor") is recorded, along with confidence interval for that percentage. A third number, called the chi-square factor, is also provided when the response varied in a sta-

CHART 1. Size of project in the study sample (all projects)

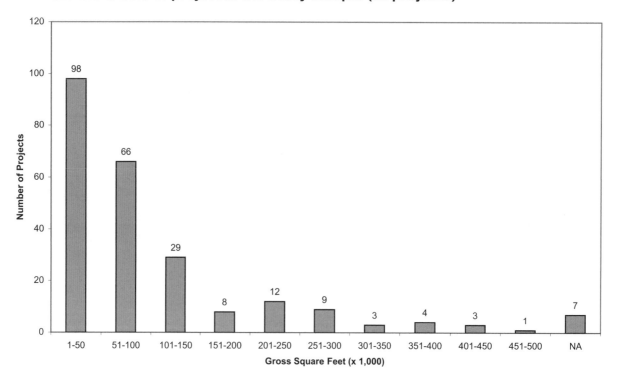

CHART 2. Size of projects in the study sample (projects ≤ 100,000 GSF)

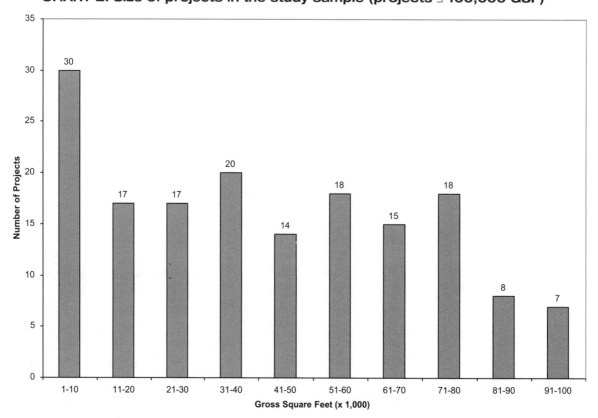

TABLE 3a. Analysis of responses to question 1 of the study survey

	Not a factor (0)		Weak Motivation (1)		(2)		Intermediate Motivation (3)		(4)		Strong Motivation (5)	
	Sample % responding affirmatively	± Confidence Interval	Sample % responding affirmatively	± Confidence Interval	Sample % responding affirmatively	± Confidence Interval	Sample % responding affirmatively	± Confidence Interval	Sample % responding affirmatively	± Confidence Interval	Sample % responding affirmatively	± Confidence Interval
Q1 Factors motivating new library space												
a Growth of library staff	38.6%	6.4%	17.9%	5.0%	7.2%	3.4%	16.1%	4.8%	10.3%	4.0%	9.9%	3.9%
chi-square factor (when significant)	*5.8*				*1.1*							
b Increase in the number of service points	42.4%	6.5%	12.1%	4.3%	9.4%	3.8%	14.7%	4.6%	11.2%	4.1%	10.3%	4.0%
chi-square factor (when significant)	*8.0*											
c Growth of the collections	8.3%	3.6%	3.5%	2.4%	4.4%	2.7%	11.0%	4.1%	16.2%	4.8%	56.6%	6.4%
chi-square factor (when significant)			*2.1*		*1.9*						*19.7*	
d Changing character of student study space needs	6.1%	3.1%	4.8%	2.8%	3.5%	2.4%	17.0%	4.9%	32.1%	5.5%	45.4%	6.4%
chi-square factor (when significant)	*1.4*		*1.7*		*2.2*						*10.3*	
e Changes in reference services	14.8%	4.7%	9.0%	3.8%	12.1%	4.3%	26.9%	5.8%	21.1%	5.4%	16.1%	4.8%
chi-square factor (when significant)							*1.3*					
f Changes in public services other than reference	13.8%	4.5%	7.1%	3.4%	7.1%	3.4%	22.2%	5.4%	23.6%	5.5%	26.2%	5.7%
chi-square factor (when significant)			*1.1*		*1.1*						*1.1*	
g Changes in or growth of library instruction programs	11.8%	4.2%	11.8%	4.2%	8.8%	3.7%	17.1%	4.9%	17.4%	5.0%	32.0%	6.1%
chi-square factor (when significant)											*2.9*	
h Changes in technical services	27.2%	5.8%	21.0%	5.3%	11.2%	4.1%	21.9%	5.4%	12.1%	4.3%	6.7%	3.3%
chi-square factor (when significant)	*1.4*										*1.2*	
i Preservation of the collections	22.2%	5.4%	12.4%	4.3%	10.7%	4.0%	20.9%	5.3%	13.8%	4.5%	21.0%	5.2%
chi-square factor (when significant)												
j Need to accommodate non-library operations	26.1%	5.7%	9.3%	3.8%	8.0%	3.5%	10.2%	3.9%	12.8%	4.4%	33.6%	6.2%
chi-square factor (when significant)	*1.1*										*3.5*	
k Building safety issues	32.3%	6.1%	15.0%	4.7%	9.7%	3.9%	19.9%	5.2%	8.8%	3.7%	14.2%	4.5%
chi-square factor (when significant)	*3.0*											
l Building mechanical systems obsolescence	32.8%	6.5%	9.1%	4.0%	0.0%	0.0%	16.2%	5.1%	14.6%	4.9%	27.3%	6.2%
chi-square factor (when significant)	*2.8*				*3.0*						*1.2*	
m Building structural problems	50.0%	6.5%	14.3%	4.6%	7.1%	3.4%	10.7%	4.1%	8.0%	3.6%	9.8%	3.9%
chi-square factor (when significant)	*13.5*											
n Dysfunctional design of previous space	11.6%	4.2%	8.9%	3.7%	5.8%	3.0%	15.6%	4.7%	17.8%	5.0%	40.4%	6.4%
chi-square factor (when significant)					*1.4*						*6.9*	

Figures in a dark gray field report responses that occur significantly more frequently than would occur in a random distribution.
Figures in a light gray field report responses that occur significantly less frequently than would occur in a random distribution.

tistically significant way from what one would expect in a random distribution of responses. The higher the chi-square factor, the more significant is the result. So, for example, Table 3a reports that 38.6% of all survey respondents who answered question 1a, about the growth of library staff, said that this was not a factor in their planning. One can be 95% confident that responses to question 1a would fall within the range of 38.6 ±6.4% for the entire population of study projects. The chi-square factor of 5.8 indicates this response differs in a highly significant way from what one would expect in a random, or chance, distribution of responses to this question. In this case, dark shading is used to indicate that the response occurs more frequently than in a random distribution; light shading used elsewhere (e.g., question 1d) indicates a response that occurs less frequently than would be expected in a random distribution.

Table 3b reports the responses to question 1 in the study survey but differs from Table 3a in sorting the responses according to the Carnegie classification of institutions. Table 3b is available in the online version of this report.

Caveat about Table 3b: Readers should understand that the relatively small number of institutions representing many of the Carnegie classification types in the study sample, as reported in Table 3b, makes inferences about the larger study population somewhat unreliable. This is indicated in the wide confidence intervals reported in this table.

Table 3c reports the responses to question 1 in the study survey but differs from Table 3a in sorting the responses according to the year when projects were completed. Table 3c is available in the online version of this report.

Caveat about Table 3c: The relatively small number of projects completed in most years in the study sample, as reported in Table 3c, makes inferences about the larger study population somewhat unreliable. This is indicated in the wide confidence intervals reported in this table.

Table 4a reports the responses to questions 2–13 in the study survey. It is similar to Table 3a except that all the questions are either explicitly or implicitly yes/no questions (rather than questions that invite responses on a scale). The percentage of all respondents to a given question who answered in the affirmative is recorded, along with a confidence interval for that percentage. A third number, called the chi-square factor, is also provided when the response varies in a statistically significant way from what one would expect in a random distribution of responses. The higher the chi-square factor, the more significant is the result. So, for example, Table 4a reports that 84.8% of all survey respondents who answered question 3a, about the systematic assessment of library operations, said that such an assessment was done. One can be 95% confident that responses to this question would fall within the range of 84.8 ±4.7% for the entire population of study projects. The chi-square factor of 28.3 indicates this response differs in a highly significant way from what one would expect in a random, or chance, distribution of responses to this ques-

TABLE 4a. Analysis of responses to questions 2–13 of the study survey

	Sample % responding affirmatively	± Confidence Interval	-square factor (when significant)
Q2 Project influenced by overall "vision" statement	65.1%	6.2%	2.7
Q3 Systematic assessment performed			
a Of library operations	84.8%	4.7%	28.3
b Of reader or user wishes	63.8%	6.3%	4.5
c Of modes of student learning	40.6%	6.4%	2.1
d Of modes of faculty teaching	31.3%	6.1%	8.2
e Of fit with the provision of other academic space	57.6%	6.5%	1.3
f Other assessments	15.6%	4.8%	27.6
Q4 Constituencies involved in planning			
a Faculty	74.6%	5.7%	14.1
b Students	51.3%	6.5%	
c Other constituencies	51.3%	6.5%	
Q5 Changes in concept of library work affected planning	73.3%	5.8%	6.4
Q6 Instruction space provided for			
a Instruction by library staff	83.5%	4.9%	26.2
b Instruction by non-library faculty	50.4%	6.5%	
c Instruction by computing services staff	33.5%	6.2%	6.4
d Teaching and curricular development	34.8%	6.2%	5.4
e Other instructional space	15.6%	4.8%	27.6
Q7 Student learning space provided that required			
a General computing laboratories	63.8%	6.3%	4.5
b Group study space	84.4%	4.8%	27.6
c Conference or other informal meeting space	63.8%	6.3%	4.5
d Other student learning space	38.8%	6.4%	2.9
Q8 Project provided for print/electronic interface	80.2%	5.2%	10.8
Q9 Project provided			
a Vending machine food and beverages	50.0%	9.0%	1.6
b Staffed food services	22.9%	7.6%	
c Other food service	27.1%	8.0%	
Q10 Project provided social space for students	46.6%	6.6%	
Q11 Project provided for future changes in space use	72.3%	5.9%	5.8
Q12 Conducted a post-occupancy assessment	15.7%	4.8%	13.7
Q13 Experience suggests need for further change	61.3%	6.4%	

Figures in a dark gray field report responses that occur significantly more frequently than would occur in a random distribution.

Figures in a light gray field report responses that occur significantly less frequently than would occur in a random distribution.

tion. In this case, dark shading is used to indicate that the response occurs more frequently than in a random distribution; light shading used elsewhere (e.g., question 3c) indicates a response that occurs less frequently than would be expected in a random distribution.

Table 4b reports the responses to questions 2–13 in the study survey but differs from Table 4a in sorting the responses according to the Carnegie classification of institutions. Table 4b is available in the online version of this report.

Caveat about Table 4b: The relatively small number of institutions representing many of the Carnegie classification types in the study sample, as reported in Table 4b, makes inferences about the larger study population somewhat unreliable. This is indicated in the wide confidence intervals reported in this table.

Table 4c reports the responses to questions 2–13 in the study survey but differs from Table 4a in sorting the responses according to the year when projects were completed. Table 4c is available in the online version of this report.

Caveat about Table 4c: The relatively small number of projects completed in most years in the study sample, as reported in Table 4c, makes inferences about the larger study population somewhat unreliable. This is indicated in the wide confidence intervals reported in this table.

Table 5 describes the distribution of projects by lead architects and of lead architects by projects in the study population.

TABLE 5. Distribution of architects

	Number	% of Total
Projects		
With an architect doing 1 library project only	256	66%
With an architect doing 2 or more library projects	132	34%
Total	*388*	*100%*
Architects		
Doing 1 library project only	256	86%
Doing 2 library projects	28	9%
Doing 3 library projects	8	3%
Doing 4 or more library projects	5	2%
Total	*297*	*100%*

Summary of Qualitative Comments Made by Survey Respondents

Comments are recorded under the survey question to which respondents attached them. This summary attempts to capture responses that are not well represented in the quantitative data or that express particularly well an idea often expressed in the comments. Where appropriate and possible, a summary analysis is offered of subjects that figure frequently in the comments. These summary comments are available in the online version of this report.

Summary and Partial Transcriptions of the Phone Interviews with Library Directors and Chief Academic Officers

As a part of this study, phone interviews were conducted with 25 library directors from institutions that responded to the study survey. Six presidents or chief academic officers (CAOs) at the institutions involved in the library director interviews were also interviewed. The summary and partial transcriptions of these interviews are available in the online version of this report. The summaries have been edited to provide anonymity. They are grouped according to the Carnegie classification of the institutions involved, as follows:

Doctoral/Research Universities—Extensive
       CAO interviews 1–4
       Library director interviews 7–14
Doctoral/Research Universities—Intensive
       CAO interview 5
       Library director interviews 15–18
Master's Colleges and Universities I
       Library director interviews 19–22
Master's Colleges and Universities II
       Library director interviews 23–24
Baccalaureate Colleges—Liberal Arts
       CAO interview 6
       Library director interviews 25–29
Baccalaureate Colleges—General
       Library director interviews 30–31

Quantitative Findings of a Survey Conducted for the Council of Independent Colleges

Tables 6a and 6b present some of the findings of a November 2001 survey of library directors and chief academic officers (CAOs) at institutions that are members of the Council of Independent Colleges (CIC). The CIC is an association of independent colleges and universities working together to support college leaders, advance institutional excellence, and enhance private higher education's contributions to society. To fulfill its mission, CIC provides ideas, resources, and services that assist institutions in improving leadership expertise, educational programs, administrative and financial performance, and institutional visibility. See http://www.cic.edu/ for more information about the CIC and for the original publication of the data reported here.

Description of the Summary Tables

- Questions 1 and 2 prompted respondents to agree or disagree with statements in a survey statement, using a five-point scale to register their views. Individual statements are listed in each row of the table followed by a set of columns that report (a) the percentage of all respondents using each of the prompted responses (**bold face**) and (b) the confidence interval for the response (*italics*). This is followed by two other statistics: (c) the median view among all responses, which is a crude measure of central tendency among the responses but the only one available for this kind of data; and (d) the results of a chi-square test for independence between the responses to each statement provided by CAOs and library directors. Where this test indicates that differences in the responses are statistically significant, the test result is reported in **bold face** followed by (e) the percentages of CAO and library director responses, provided to facilitate understanding of how they differ.

Look, for instance, at question 1.04:

(a) Of the 101 respondents, 70% strongly agree with the statement that library staff should provide in-class library instruction; 24% agree with this assertion, while 4% are undecided or have no opinion. Two percent of the respondents disagree with the statement, but none strongly disagrees with it.

(b) Each of these response values is followed by a confidence interval. In the case of the 70% who strongly agree, for instance, one can be confident that 95% of the time between 60% and 80% (i.e., 70% plus or minus 10%) of the larger population of all CAOs and library directors at CIC institutions (represented by the sample who responded to this statement) would strongly agree with this statement.

(c) The median view among all respondents indicates strong agreement that professional library staff should provide in-class library instruction.

(d) While the median view (a relatively crude measure) of both CAOs and library directors is the same, the chi-square test for difference (a more discriminating measure) indicates that CAOs as a group hold this view less strongly than do library directors.

(e) This difference is evident in the large percentage of "agree" responses among CAOs, compared to the small percentage of "agree" responses among library directors.

- Question 3 prompted respondents to assign priority, on a three-point scale, to several activities that might be accommodated in new library space. The rest of the table functions the same way as the table for questions 1 and 2.

Look, for instance, at question 3.14. Of the 101 respondents, 25% would give high priority to providing new library space to student socializing (without food), while 41% of the respondents would give medium priority to this need and 35% would give it low priority. In the case of the 25% who regard such socializing as a high priority, for instance, one can be confident that 95% of the time between 17% and 33% (i.e., 25% plus or minus 8%) of the larger population of all CAOs and library directors at CIC institutions would strongly agree with this statement. The median view among all respondents is that providing new library space for student socializing has a medium priority. CAOs and library directors, however, have decidedly different views of this matter, as evident in the comparatively large percentage of library directors assigning high priority to this need and the comparatively low percentage who regard it as a low priority.

TABLE 6a. Survey of library directors and chief academic officers at CIC institutions: questions 1 and 2

	All responses										Median view among all responses (n=101)	Chi-square test for independence (alpha = 0.05, df = 4)	Selected CAO responses					Selected Lib Dir responses				
	Strongly agree	+/- conf	Agree	+/- conf	No opinion/undecided	+/- conf	Disagree	+/- conf	Strongly disagree	+/- conf			Strongly agree	Agree	No opinion/undecided	Disagree	Strongly disagree	Strongly agree	Agree	No opinion/undecided	Disagree	Strongly disagree
1.00 Roles of professional library staff																						
1.01 Provide reference service	93%	5%	7%	5%	0%	na	0%	na	0%	na	Strongly agree	0.00										
1.02 Select material for collections	78%	8%	18%	8%	1%	2%	3%	3%	0%	na	Strongly agree	8.57										
1.03 Provide library instruction	91%	6%	8%	6%	0%	2%	0%	2%	0%	2%	Strongly agree	1.01										
1.04 Provide in-class library instruction	70%	9%	24%	8%	4%	4%	2%	4%	0%	3%	Strongly agree	**10.79**	57%	34%	5%	4%	0%	87%	11%	2%	0%	0%
1.05 Advise faculty on IT and information resources	51%	10%	32%	8%	13%	7%	4%	7%	0%	4%	Strongly agree	4.20										
1.06 Offer technical support to faculty in the classroom	13%	7%	19%	8%	22%	8%	40%	10%	7%	5%	No opinion/undecided	1.44										
1.07 Serve as course instructors	33%	9%	37%	10%	23%	8%	7%	8%	0%	5%	Agree	4.12										
1.08 Serve on technology planning committees	64%	9%	32%	9%	4%	4%	0%	4%	0%	na	Strongly agree	**14.33**	48%	46%	5%	0%	0%	84%	13%	2%	0%	0%
1.09 Serve on curriculum committees	52%	10%	27%	10%	11%	9%	8%	5%	2%	3%	Strongly agree	**14.12**	38%	32%	18%	9%	4%	71%	20%	2%	7%	0%
1.10 Serve on distance education planning committees	49%	10%	28%	10%	18%	8%	2%	8%	3%	3%	Agree	**25.28**	29%	31%	31%	4%	5%	74%	23%	2%	0%	0%
1.11 Serve on college planning and budget committees	50%	10%	37%	10%	10%	6%	3%	3%	10%	6%	Agree	**11.10**	36%	45%	13%	5%	2%	67%	27%	7%	0%	0%
1.12 Serve on college governance committees	45%	10%	32%	10%	13%	9%	9%	6%	1%	2%	Agree	8.43										
2.00 Existing library space should support																						
2.01 Shelving library collections	93%	5%	7%	5%	0%	na	0%	na	0%	na	Strongly agree	0.77										
2.02 Reference assistance	95%	4%	5%	4%	0%	na	0%	na	0%	na	Strongly agree	4.23										
2.03 Reserved readings for courses	90%	6%	10%	6%	0%	na	0%	na	0%	na	Strongly agree	1.02										
2.04 Student study space BEFORE midnight	87%	7%	13%	7%	0%	na	0%	na	0%	na	Strongly agree	0.23										
2.05 Student study space AFTER midnight	18%	8%	17%	8%	19%	8%	33%	9%	14%	7%	No opinion/undecided	1.78										
2.06 E-mail services for students and faculty	21%	8%	27%	8%	14%	9%	31%	9%	8%	5%	No opinion/undecided	**17.17**	13%	20%	21%	41%	5%	31%	36%	4%	18%	11%
2.07 General computing laboratories for students	15%	7%	39%	10%	16%	10%	26%	9%	4%	4%	Agree	6.56										
2.08 Faculty consulting with students	15%	7%	37%	9%	26%	9%	20%	9%	1%	2%	Agree	**12.40**	13%	25%	38%	25%	0%	18%	51%	16%	13%	2%
2.09 General faculty offices	2%	3%	5%	3%	26%	9%	50%	10%	18%	8%	Disagree	5.53										
2.10 Instruction in information literacy	75%	8%	24%	8%	1%	2%	0%	2%	0%	na	Strongly agree	5.94										
2.11 General classroom instruction	2%	3%	18%	3%	27%	9%	42%	10%	12%	6%	Disagree	7.65										
2.12 Collaborative learning among students	43%	10%	43%	10%	11%	7%	3%	3%	1%	2%	Agree	**23.89**	23%	54%	18%	5%	0%	67%	29%	2%	0%	2%
2.13 Center for innovation in teaching and learning	16%	7%	28%	9%	35%	9%	20%	8%	2%	3%	No opinion/undecided	**10.56**	7%	25%	43%	21%	4%	27%	31%	24%	18%	0%
2.14 Socializing among students (without food service)	16%	7%	42%	10%	16%	7%	18%	7%	8%	5%	Agree	**13.03**	7%	36%	20%	25%	11%	28%	51%	12%	9%	0%
2.15 Socializing among students (with food service)	6%	5%	25%	9%	22%	9%	29%	9%	18%	8%	No opinion/undecided	**15.00**	2%	15%	22%	40%	22%	11%	38%	22%	16%	13%
2.16 Equipment and staff for AV support of teaching	27%	9%	32%	9%	17%	9%	21%	8%	3%	3%	Agree	**10.58**	24%	27%	25%	24%	0%	31%	38%	7%	18%	7%
2.17 Computing staff and equipment	7%	5%	22%	8%	26%	9%	36%	9%	10%	6%	No opinion/undecided	8.33										
2.18 Exhibition of museum and other non-library material	21%	8%	48%	10%	16%	10%	14%	7%	1%	2%	Agree	9.43										

TABLE 6b. Survey of library directors and chief academic officers at CIC institutions: question 3

	All responses						Median view among all responses (n=101)	Chi-square test for independence (alpha = 0.05, df = 2)	Selected CAO responses			Selected Lib Dir Responses		
	High priority	Plus/minus confidence	Medium Priority	Plus/minus confidence	Low priority	Plus/minus confidence			High priority	Medium Priority	Low priority	High priority	Medium Priority	Low priority
3.00 Priority uses of additional library space														
3.01 Shelving library collections	67%	9%	28%	9%	5%	4%	High priority	0.43						
3.02 Reference assistance	73%	9%	22%	8%	5%	4%	High priority	3.64						
3.03 Reserved readings for courses	46%	10%	35%	9%	20%	8%	Medium priority	3.88						
3.04 Student study space BEFORE midnight	75%	9%	17%	9%	8%	6%	High priority	4.86						
3.05 Student study space AFTER midnight	24%	8%	26%	9%	50%	10%	Low priority	0.80						
3.06 E-mail services for students and faculty	16%	7%	30%	9%	54%	10%	Low priority	21.93	2%	29%	70%	34%	32%	34%
3.07 General computing laboratories for students	25%	8%	44%	10%	32%	9%	Medium priority	5.10						
3.08 Faculty consulting with students	14%	7%	47%	10%	40%	10%	Medium priority	11.63	5%	43%	52%	24%	51%	24%
3.09 General faculty offices	0%	na	14%	na	86%	7%	Low priority	0.97						
3.10 Instruction in information literacy	79%	8%	21%	8%	0%	na	High priority	13.17	66%	34%	0%	96%	4%	0%
3.11 General classroom instruction	6%	5%	30%	9%	64%	9%	Low priority	0.82						
3.12 Collaborative learning among students	51%	10%	39%	10%	10%	6%	High priority	6.27	41%	45%	14%	64%	31%	4%
3.13 Center for innovation in teaching and learning	30%	9%	42%	10%	29%	9%	Medium priority	10.88	18%	43%	39%	44%	40%	16%
3.14 Socializing among students (without food service)	25%	8%	41%	10%	35%	9%	Medium priority	18.25	9%	45%	46%	44%	36%	20%
3.15 Socializing among students (with food service)	16%	7%	34%	9%	50%	10%	Low priority	14.70	4%	36%	61%	31%	31%	38%
3.16 Equipment and staff for AV support of teaching	36%	9%	34%	9%	31%	9%	Medium priority	6.44	25%	38%	38%	49%	29%	22%
3.17 Computing staff and equipment	17%	7%	31%	9%	52%	10%	Low priority	8.72	7%	32%	61%	29%	29%	42%
3.18 Exhibition of museum and other non-library material	32%	9%	47%	10%	20%	8%	Medium priority	0.71						

PART 3:
RESEARCH METHODOLOGY

This part of the report describes the research methodologies used in the study. The intention is to enable readers to judge how reliable the study's findings are and to explore further the implications of the study's data.

Described here are the methodologies used in (1) compiling the investment parameters reported in Figure 1 and Table 1; (2) the survey of academic institutions that undertook renovations and additions to existing libraries or built new libraries between 1992 and 2001; and (3) the phone interviews of library directors and academic officers at a number of institutions that responded to the survey. For information about the methodology used in the Council of Independent Colleges (CIC) survey of library directors and chief academic officers, see section 4 of the report on that survey, which is available at http://www.cic.org/projects_services/index.asp.

Investment Parameters

Information from 1992 through 2001 on several factors—e.g., number of academic library projects, total cost, total gross square feet (GSF)—were extracted and summed from the reports on library capital projects reported annually in the December issue of *Library Journal*. Ten-year means and standard deviations were calculated for each factor, as were the z scores for each annual statistic. These z scores indicate that all the annual statistics fall well within a normal distribution of values. Note that the total current dollar costs, as reported in the *Library Journal*, were converted to total real dollar costs using the index values of the gross domestic product published by the U.S. Bureau of Economic Analysis. This conversion was done to permit comparisons across a ten-year period.

Survey of Academic Institutions Undertaking Library Construction between 1992 and 2001

Scope of the Survey

The survey focused on academic library projects (new buildings, renovations, and additions) undertaken in the United States primarily between 1992 and 2001.

- Academic libraries are of interest to the study's sponsor, the Council on Library and Information Resources. They have a distinctive institutional setting and clientele, and the investigator has some familiarity with academic libraries, having worked most of his professional life in such libraries.
- Projects in the 1990s were completed at a time of significant pedagogical and technological change in higher education. Personal and institutional memories of projects completed earlier than 1992 are likely to have dimmed.
- Imaginative, forward-looking libraries were built in many countries other than the United States in the 1990s. This study nonetheless confined itself to those built in the United States to simplify the identification of projects, to keep the number of projects manageable, to facilitate the interviews (which could be done in one language and in only four time zones), and to avoid contextual issues (e.g., the kind of national planning represented by the Follett report in the United Kingdom) with which the investigator is not familiar.

Database of Projects Undertaken between 1992 and 2001

A list of additions, renovations, and new building projects was compiled from the lists of libraries undertaking such construction published annually in the December issue of *Library Journal*. Other projects identified in a literature search were added, yielding a list of 443 projects. The intention was to identify projects completed between 1992 and 2001, but inaccuracies in reporting dates and other factors resulted in the inclusion of a small number of projects completed or ongoing in 2002.

For each project, the following information was compiled:

- the institution's name and mailing address
- the institution's Carnegie classification
- the name of the library involved
- the name of and contact information for the library director responsible for the project
- the nature of the project (i.e., renovation, addition, or new construction), the size of the project in gross square feet, and its completion date
- the name of the lead architect for the project (this information about architects provides the basis for Figure 7 in part 1 and Table 5 in part 2 of the report)

Survey respondents were asked to review the database information about their project and to correct any mistakes.

The letter inviting library directors to participate in the study is available in the online version of this report.

Survey Instrument

Council on Library and Information Resources
Survey of Recent Library Space Planning Practices

Thank you for responding to the following questions regarding your experience in library planning. The Council on Library and Information Resources greatly values your assistance with this project.

If you have any questions about this CLIR survey, please get in touch with Scott Bennett at: 2scottb@prairienet.org or at 217-367-9896.

PROJECT IDENTIFICATION

Please enter in the following box the questionnaire number given at the beginning of the letter you received inviting your participation in this survey. If your letter had more than one number identifying different projects, please fill out a separate response for each different project.

Questionnaire number xxx supplied on Web form

PROJECT DATA

A literature review suggests that the following library has, in the last ten years, been built, added to, or renovated. If the project information supplied below is inaccurate or incomplete, please make the necessary changes.

Institution name: (*supplied on Web form*)

Library name: (*supplied on Web form*)

Date completed: (*supplied on Web form*)

Approximate size of the project (x 1,000 GSF): (*supplied on Web form*)

Principal architect: (*supplied on Web form*)

If *all* of the information supplied above is incorrect, please delete it and submit the questionnaire without answering the remaining questions.

FACTORS MOTIVATING NEW LIBRARY SPACE

1. Which of the following considerations primarily motivated your library renovation/construction project? Please indicate the strength of motivation for as many considerations as apply. Use the last column to indicate the consideration was not a factor.

	Strong Motivation 5	4	Intermediate Motivation 3	2	Weak Motivation 1	Not a Factor 0
• Growth of library staff (either librarians or support staff)	❏	❏	❏	❏	❏	❏
• Increase in the number of library service points	❏	❏	❏	❏	❏	❏
• Growth of the collections	❏	❏	❏	❏	❏	❏
• Changing character of student study space needs	❏	❏	❏	❏	❏	❏
• Changes in reference services	❏	❏	❏	❏	❏	❏
• Changes in public services other than reference (e.g., circulation, ILL, general changes in information technology)	❏	❏	❏	❏	❏	❏
• Changes in or growth of library instruction programs (including the need for electronic classrooms for library instruction)	❏	❏	❏	❏	❏	❏
• Changes in technical services and other library operations with limited interactions with readers	❏	❏	❏	❏	❏	❏
• Preservation of the collections	❏	❏	❏	❏	❏	❏
• Need to accommodate operations not previously housed in the library (e.g., computing centers and other IT operations, audiovisual services, teaching and learning centers, writing centers, general classrooms or offices)	❏	❏	❏	❏	❏	❏
• Building safety issues	❏	❏	❏	❏	❏	❏
• Building mechanical systems Obsolescence	❏	❏	❏	❏	❏	❏
• Building structural problems (including earthquake protection)	❏	❏	❏	❏	❏	❏
• Dysfunctional design of previous space	❏	❏	❏	❏	❏	❏

• Other considerations (please specify):

_____

_____

_____

PROCESS FOR ARTICULATING YOUR GOALS

2. Was the design of your project meaningfully influenced by an overall "vision" statement, or similar document, regarding your library's mission and services?

Yes ❏   No ❏

3. Did you undertake any of the formal, systematic assessments of your needs in the following list before starting to specify the technical program for your project?

Please check box to indicate "yes" for as many as apply:
❑ Assessment of library operations (e.g., occupancy rates, service counts, collection growth rates, library staff work flows, survey of building conditions)
❑ Assessment of reader or user wishes
❑ Assessment of modes of student learning
❑ Assessment of modes of faculty teaching
❑ Assessment of the library as one element in the larger provision of academic space on campus
❑ Other assessment activities (please specify):
_____
_____
_____

4. Which of the following reader constituencies were significantly involved in planning your project?

Please check box to indicate "yes" for as many as apply:
❑ Faculty
❑ Students
❑ Other (specify): _____

5. Did important changes in the concept of library work, including any expansion of staff functions or responsibilities, affect your library space planning?

Yes ❑   No ❑

If yes, please briefly describe that reconceptualization: _____
_____
_____
_____

6. Did your project provide significant instructional space for:

Please check box to indicate "yes" for as many as apply:
❑ Instructional activities conducted by library staff (either librarians or support staff)
❑ Instructional activities conducted by nonlibrary faculty or graduate students
❑ Instructional activities conducted by computing services staff
❑ Teaching and curricular development, or other faculty development activities
❑ Other instructional space (please specify):
_____
_____
_____

7. Did your project provide significant space for student learning activities requiring:

Please check box to indicate "yes" for as many as apply:
❑ General computing laboratories
❑ Group study space for students
❑ Conference or other informal meeting space for faculty and students
❑ Other student learning space (please specify):
_____
_____
_____

8. Did your project provide space to improve for readers the interface between print and electronic information resources? A possible example would be online catalog workstations placed in the book stacks.

Yes ❑   No ❑

If yes, please specify the way the space is used:

_____
_____
_____

9. Did your project provide for:

Please check box to indicate "yes" for as many as apply:
❑ Vending machine food and beverage services
❑ Staffed food services
❑ Other food service (specify): _____

10. Did your project provide social space for students (other than food service and group study spaces)?

Yes ❑   No ❑

If yes, please describe the space:

_____
_____
_____

11. Did your project self-consciously allow for future changes in the use of library space, even those you could not confidently forecast?

Yes ❑   No ❑

If yes, please briefly describe your strategy of accommodating such change:

_____
_____
_____

POST-OCCUPANCY ACTIVITES

12. Once your project was finished and the space occupied, did you conduct a formal post-occupancy assessment of how well the project meets your needs?

Yes ❑   No ❑

13. Has the experience of working in your new project suggested the need for further significant change in library space?

Yes ❑   No ❑

14. Would you be willing to be interviewed by the CLIR project investigator seeking a more detailed understanding of your project?

Yes ❑   No ❑

If yes, please provide the following information:

Name: _____

Title: _____

E-mail: _____

Phone: _____

You might wish to review your responses before sending them to CLIR. You may change any response by deleting it and providing a new answer.

When you have completed the questionnaire, you may submit it to CLIR by clicking on the following Submit button.

Submit button

THANK YOU VERY MUCH FOR YOUR ASSISTANCE.

Methods of Analyzing Survey Data

The survey posed four kinds of questions:

- Questions 2, 5, 8, and 10–13: These questions invited a single affirmative response. Every affirmative implied a reciprocal negative.
- Questions 3, 4, 6, and 7: These three- to six-element questions invited multiple affirmative responses. An affirmative response to one element in these questions did not exclude an affirmative response to other elements but did, by inference, imply a reciprocal negative for the element in question. The individual elements in these questions could therefore be treated as if they were "yes/no" questions comparable to questions 2, 5, 8, and 10–13.
- Question 9: This three-element question was treated as if an affirmative response to one element excluded an affirmative response to other elements.
- Question 1: This 14-element question invited affirmative responses weighted (on a six-point scale) by intensity. The intensity rating for any given element carried no implication for the rating of other elements.

Excluding the "other" responses, there were a total of 114 question categories to track for each survey returned and reported in Tables 3a and 4a. When the responses were analyzed by ungrouped and grouped Carnegie classification numbers (Tables 3b and 4b), there were 1,596 question categories to track. When the responses were analyzed by project-completion year (Tables 3c and 4c), there were 1,254 question categories to track.

There were 240 usable, nonduplicative responses to the survey, yielding a 54% rate of return. The study considered the 443 libraries identified in its database as the study's population, while it took the 240 survey responses as a study sample representing the study population.

In the ensuing description of statistical methods, the following terms are used:

- "Question" identifies a question as it was presented to readers of the survey—e.g., question 1 about several different factors that motivated projects
- "Question element" identifies a particular factor in the question— e.g., the growth of library staff in question 1 or the "yes" option in several other questions
- "Question category" or "category" identifies the intensity response or the yes/no response used by the respondent for each question element—e.g., the growth of library staff identified as a weak motivator, or a "no" response about post-occupancy assessment.

For all questions, the proportion (P) of affirmative responses to each question element was determined and a corresponding confidence interval for P calculated. This confidence interval indicates the range (reported as plus-or-minus percentage points) within which responses for the study population are likely to vary from the study sample (i.e., P) in 95 out of 100 cases.

The chi-square test was then applied in the following ways to determine whether differences in P were statistically significant.

- In Tables 3a and 4a, actual P responses were compared to a random (i.e., uniform) set of responses. For question 1 (Table 3a) "random response" was defined as the total number of responses divided by six, the number of question categories (i.e., random response = mean response). To determine the mean or random response rates in the other questions (Table 4a), the total number of responses was divided by 2 for the "yes" and "no" response categories actually provided in questions 2, 5, 8, and 10–13 or implied for each of the elements in questions 3, 4, 6, and 7. For questions 3, 4, 6, and 7, the total number of responses had to be inferred because it could not be observed directly (that is, an affirmative response to one element in these questions did not exclude an affirmative response to other elements). The inferred number of responses was defined as the mean of the actual responses to questions 2, 5, 8, 9, and 10–13 (where an affirmative response to one element did exclude an affirmative response to other elements). This mean was 224, suggesting that 224 out of a possible 240 respondents (93.3%) actually answered the questions at issue here.

- In the analysis of P responses grouped by Carnegie classification type (Tables 3b and 4b) and by projection-completion year (Tables 3c and 4c), the actual responses by institutional type were compared not with random responses but with the actual responses for the sample, considered as a whole (i.e., the Tables 3a and 3b results).

- Where differences in response were statistically significant, that fact was registered in Tables 3a–c and 4a–c by the use of bold type and by a ratio called the chi-square factor. This factor equals the results of the chi-square test divided by the value of the critical region appropriate to the given question element (different elements require the use of different degrees of freedom in determining the critical region). In effect, the chi-square factor indicates how many times the results of the chi-square test exceeded the value of the critical region for that test. This use of the chi-square factor provides a single scale for comparing responses that require somewhat different underlying values in testing for statistical significance. Hence, any chi-square factor value of ≤ 1 falls outside the critical region and is not statistically significant. Any factor value of ≥ 1 falls within the critical region and is statistically significant. The higher the chi-square factor value is above 1, the less likely it is that the response could have happened by chance.

- See the online version of this report for some additional measures of statistical significance provided in Tables 3b–c and 4b–c, along with a note about the statistical validity of these tables.

Interviews of Library Directors and Chief Academic Officers at Some Institutions that Responded to the Survey

Selection of Library Directors to Participate in Phone Interviews

The identification of persons to interview was a multistep process. No attempt was made to identify a random, stratified sample from the survey respondents, but an attempt was made to include a variety of types of institutions in the interviews that roughly paralleled the variety of institutions in the study sample.

- As a first step, the number of interviews to be sought at various institutional types (using the Carnegie Classification) was determined, based on the proportion of institutional types responding to the survey: Doctoral/Research Universities—Extensive (nine interviews); Doctoral/Research Universities—Intensive (four interviews); Master's Colleges and Universities I (seven interviews); Master's Colleges and Universities II (one interview); Baccalaureate Colleges—Liberal Arts (five interviews); Baccalaureate Colleges—General (two interviews); Associate's Colleges (two interviews). This institutional profile for the interviews approximates that of the study sample, except that Doctoral/Research Universities—Extensive are under-represented by one interview and Baccalaureate Colleges—Liberal Arts are overrepresented by one interview. This slight adjustment was made with the hope of securing more informative interview results.

- All respondents who offered three or more comments in responding to the survey were selected for interviews, on the supposition that they were most strongly engaged with the topics being investigated. In fact, these respondents often had thoughtful, provocative things to say in their survey comments.

- All the respondents who offered two comments in responding to the survey were sorted into institution types (using the Carnegie classification). Most of these respondents could be included in the interviews within the limits set for the various institutional types. No individual with particularly interesting or provocative comments in the survey was omitted.

- A small number of Doctoral/Research Universities—Extensive, Master's Colleges and Universities I, Baccalaureate Colleges—Liberal Arts, and Baccalaureate Colleges—General were selected from the list of survey respondents, sorted by institutional types. In selecting these institutions, at attempt was made to balance public and private institutions and to secure some geographical spread.

- All respondents identified in this way had indicated, in survey question 14, a willingness to participate in a follow-up interview. Not all respondents so identified were in fact willing to be interviewed, so the institutional profile of completed interviews did not match the intended profile. Notably, there were no interviews of library directors from Associate's Colleges.

In the event, the study included 25 interviews with library directors. Some directors asked colleagues to substitute for them in these interviews; others asked colleagues to join them during the interviews.

Questions Posed in the Phone Interviews of Library Directors

Library directors received the following set of interview questions well before their actual interview. They were asked, as part of the scheduling process, to identify which of these questions would be most pertinent to their project. The scripts for each interview included the questions so identified as well as other questions of particular interest to the investigator. Actual interviews often varied somewhat from the prepared scripts.

INTERVIEW QUESTIONS

1. Survey results indicate that meeting the space needs of library instruction, especially that for electronic classrooms, was a major motivator of library capital projects.
- Was this a major motivator for your project?
- Aside from electronic classrooms, how if at all did your project strengthen your library instruction program?

2. Survey results indicate that accommodating changing patterns of student study, especially as regards group study, was a major motivator of library capital projects.
- Was this a major motivator for your project?
- Aside from group study space, how if at all did your project respond to student needs for study space?

3. Though not explicitly inquired about, respondent comments on the survey indicate that the needs of special collections sometimes were a major motivator of library capital projects.
- Was that so for your project?
- If it was, what conception of these often less frequently used and/or relatively narrowly defined collections succeeded in attracting support for your project?

4. Survey results indicate that the need to provide shelving for collections was a major motivator of library capital projects.
- Was this a major motivator for your project?
- Do you expect shelving to be a major motivator of capital spending for your library over the next 30 years?
- Is the long-term preservation of your print collections a major factor in the design of your library's shelving?
- If preservation and access values were in conflict in the design of shelving space (e.g., lighting and temperature conditions ideal for books but less than ideal for readers), which value would prevail?
- Have you considered a satellite, high-efficiency shelving facility for your library?
- Does the availability of electronic journals and books figure ex-

plicitly in your thinking about future shelving needs? Have you quantified the likely impact of electronic materials on your future need for shelving?

- Does the availability of print material through consortial arrangements figure explicitly in your thinking about future shelving needs? Have you quantified the likely impact of consortial access arrangements on your future need for shelving?

5. Survey results indicate that "vision statements" were often critically important in guiding library capital projects.
- Was that so for your project?
- How was the vision statement developed?
- What relationship did the vision statement have to formal, systematic needs assessments?
- Might you share the vision statement with me?

6. Survey results indicate that while changes in technology frequently drive the need to reconfigure library space for specific services and operations, there is relatively little fundamental rethinking of the need for and uses of library space. Aside from the omnipresent computer (often presented in clusters), group study space, and electronic classrooms, library space today has much the same character and basic function as library space built a generation ago.
- Do you agree with this characterization of your project? If not, how would you modify it?
- Should we expect major changes in library space design to evolve in largely incremental and experimental ways, building on what we know has worked well in the past?
- Are there opportunities to break with an evolutionary process of library design and adopt more radical, revolutionary, and possibly risky views of what library space should be?

7. Survey results indicate that the formal, systematic assessment of specific departmental operations sometimes plays a significant role in formulating library capital projects and in justifying them to academic and funding bodies. Otherwise, the formal assessment of readers' wishes, of student and faculty academic needs, and of library space as one element in the campus-wide provision of academic space is rarely done. By contrast, consultation with library users, as distinguished from formal needs assessment, is quite frequent. But respondents often comment that such consultation is largely routine in nature and rarely if ever decisively important in project design.
- Was your project completed without any significant, formal, and systematic assessment of reader needs?
- If so, would your project have been strengthened by such an assessment of (for instance) student learning behaviors, faculty teaching strategies, the campus-wide provision of study space, or the interrelations of social space and study space? Why (or why not) would assessments of this sort have strengthened your project? Why was such assessment not done, if it would have been helpful?

- Was consultation with faculty and students decisively important to specific design decisions made for your project?
- Faculty members are quite frequently consulted about library projects. In your case, was that done for reasons relating to the specific teaching and research functions of faculty, as distinguished from reasons relating to the weight of faculty opinion generally in setting campus goals and priorities?
- Research indicates that faculty visit and use library space much less frequently than do students, yet consultation with students about library design happens much less frequently than with faculty. Was this the case in your project? If so, does this fact reflect the relative weight of faculty and student opinion in setting priorities on your campus? Does it reflect some other consideration?
- In consulting with faculty and students about your project, what did you aim for beyond "buy in" and "political support" among decision makers?

8. Aside from the assessment and consultation activities just discussed, how would you describe the process for coming to agreement on your library project

- as regards its programmatic goals, especially any goals rooted in the identified needs of students and faculty as distinguished from the operational goals of library units?
- as regards your project's relative priority among competing campus projects?
- as regards funding?

9. How long did it take to move your project from (a) its first formulation for members of the campus community beyond librarians to (b) the institutional funding of the project? Did the length of project gestation bear on your decisions regarding formal, systematic needs assessment and consultation with various reader constituencies?

10. Survey results indicate that formal post-occupancy studies are infrequently undertaken to measure the success of library capital projects.

- Was that the case for your project?
- If so, what other methods (if any) did you use to assess the success of your project?
- Has your assessment (whether formal or informal) of the success of your project changed over time?
- If you would now do your project differently in some significant way, did you know at the time that the project design should be changed or did you discover that only afterwards?

11. Was the inclusion in your project of some function not administered by the library (e.g., some function related to information technology services) critical to its conception and success? If so, what was that function? Do you regard the inclusion of that nonlibrary function as a strategically important alliance for the library or as a

"marriage of convenience" useful in moving your project forward?

12. If you had to reduce to just one factor the value your library creates for your campus, would timely and convenient access to information resources be that value?
- If not this, what would be the single most important value your library creates?
- Where would you rank instruction in the identification and effective use of information resources among the values created by your library?

13. What questions, beyond those posed above, would help to understand the planning process for your project, especially as regards the identification of the teaching and learning functions of library space?

Phone Interview Procedures for Library Directors
See the online version of this report for a description of the phone interview procedures used in the study.

Selection of Chief Academic Officers to Participate in Study Interviews
Library directors were asked about the participation in their library projects of their chief academic officers and other academic officers. Interviews were sought with all such individuals identified as having a significant, substantive impact on the project beyond the typical responsibilities of setting the priority of the library project amid competing campus projects, establishing project budget parameters, and fund raising. The study included six interviews with chief academic officers and other administrative officers.

Questions Posed in the Phone Interviews of Chief Academic Officers
The e-mail message inviting chief academic officers and other administrative officers to participate in the interviews included the following paragraphs. Actual interviews often varied somewhat from the script.

SCRIPT FOR CHIEF ACADEMIC OFFICER INTERVIEWS
The following questions all ask about the same thing: the role of the chief academic officer in ensuring that library space is as responsive as possible to the institution's teaching and learning missions. Our conversation could begin with any one of these questions, or with some other matter that seems more salient to you.

1. Chief academic officers typically play several managerial roles in library space planning. They are involved in determining the priority of library projects among other campus projects, setting the timetable for projects, establishing project budgets and securing funds, and managing the political process needed to initiate and complete capital projects. What other roles, if any, did you play in planning for

[project name]? Did any part of your involvement in library space planning focus specifically on possibilities for advancing your core concerns with teaching and learning?

2. In setting priorities for the project, how did you balance responding to long-accumulating space problems (e.g., lack of shelving space, obsolescent mechanical systems) with opportunities to enhance teaching and learning (e.g., group study space, electronic classrooms)?

3. Most library planning efforts involve consultation with students and faculty. This consultation seeks to understand the operational needs of these readers (e.g., students' seating preferences); gain buy-in for the project, especially from faculty; and manage the political process of deciding on project priorities. How well does this consultation process identify opportunities for library space to advance strongly the institution's fundamental missions in teaching and learning? Can this consultation process be improved? Are there other steps—such as formal assessments of modes of student teaching and faculty teaching—that might increase the likelihood that library space will advance the institution's teaching and learning missions?

4. Aside from the consultation process, it appears that college and university academic officers depend heavily on the good professional judgment of librarians, especially the library director, to guide library space planning. How well does this dependence advance opportunities for library space to serve the institution's fundamental missions in teaching and learning?

5. Chief academic officers are involved in planning for all sorts of capital projects. Does library space planning offer you distinctive opportunities to advance the teaching and learning missions of your institution? What is distinctive, if anything, about your involvement in library space planning?

The phone interview procedures for chief academic officers and other administrative officers were essentially the same as for library directors.

PART 4:
SELECTED READINGS

Agreat many excellent publications are available to persons who manage planning for library space and for the numerous consulting, construction, and other activities that yield new or renovated libraries. Most publications address the needs of those who already know "what" they want to do and need help in understanding "how" to achieve their purposes.

The following list, by contrast, provides some initial guidance to those who are primarily concerned with "what" their library project should be, especially in relation to the fundamental learning and teaching missions of the institution their library serves. The list is meant to be suggestive and is by no means exhaustive.

Bazillion, Richard J., and Connie L. Braun. 2001. *Academic Libraries as High-Tech Gateways: A Guide to Design & Space Decisions.* **2nd ed. Chicago: American Library Association.**

Bazillion and Braun provide an excellent bibliography and, in chapter 1, a good survey of recent thinking about the forces of change in librarianship. Chapter 6, "The Library as a Teaching and Learning Instrument" (pp. 171-199), focuses primarily on the library as a teaching place and does not address student learning behaviors as a possible driver of library design. The authors concentrate on the library as a home for technology and instruction in the use of technology, including such spaces as electronic classrooms, information arcades, and academic technology centers.

Bechtel, Joan M. 1986. Conversation, A New Paradigm for Librarianship? *College & Research Libraries* **47: 219-224.**

See the Bruffee entry, below, for an account of this article.

Brand, Steward. 1994. *How Buildings Learn: What Happens after They're Built.* **New York: Viking.**

This is a deservedly well-known account of how those who occupy buildings reshape the purposes of those buildings over time and of how architectural design can facilitate or hinder the ineluctable process of change. See also Wiley, below.

Bruffee, Kenneth A. 1999. *Collaborative Learning: Higher Education, Interdependence, and the Authority of Knowledge.* **2nd ed. Baltimore: Johns Hopkins University Press.**

Bruffee describes a foundational or cognitive view of knowledge as believing that "knowledge is an entity formalized by the individual mind and verified against reality" (p. 180)—that knowledge in this sense is founded in external reality as engaged by individual intelligence. Foundational views of knowledge underscore the authority of the teacher. By contrast, nonfoundational views hold that knowledge is constructed by people acting within communities.

> Knowledge is a community project. People construct knowledge working together in groups, interdependently. All knowledge is therefore the 'property' not of an individual person but of some community or other, the community that constructed it in the language spoken by the members of that community (pp. 294-295).

> We learned a lot from reading, of course. That was because reading is one way to join new communities, the ones represented by the authors of the texts we read. By reading, we acquire fluency in the language of the text and make it our own. Library stacks, from this perspective, are not a repository; they are a crowd (pp. 8-9).

> Involving local libraries and librarians as part of a "distance learning" system can . . . [turn the enterprise into something like the experience of residential college and university education] only if the program revises the ubiquitous foundational understanding of what learning is and what libraries are. . . . Joan M. Bechtel has argued the position, for example, that the most appropriate "new paradigm for librarianship" is "conversation." The traditional views of a library as a "warehouse for storing books" and as "the heart of the college and university" or "the center of our intellectual life," Bechtel says, are equally archaic. Storing books, she points out, is only one of many services libraries provide these days. The heart of the intellectual life of a college and university is more likely to be, among other places, in "a group of friends who meet regularly for study and discussion." Instead, Bechtel says, what libraries do is "collect people and ideas" and "facilitate conversation among people. . . . The preservation of crucial conversations [as recorded in the published record], the first task of libraries, [serves] not

only to preserve the record, but more important to ensure the continuation of significant conversations already in progress" (p. 130).

Bruffee observes that libraries are beginning to reflect this purpose in the provision of what he calls "conversation rooms," more commonly called group study spaces. Notably, Bruffee recognizes the importance of learning spaces and includes a brief appendix, Architecture and Classroom Design (pp. 259-261).

Buildings, Books, and Bytes: Libraries and Communities in the Digital Age. A Report on the Public's Opinion of Library Leaders' Vision for the Future. **1996. Washington, D.C.: Benton Foundation.**

The report is primarily concerned with public libraries and public support for them. In summarizing an opinion survey, the report says, "Americans value maintaining and building public library buildings. Americans support using library budgets to preserve and erect library buildings, placing this activity third in the poll's rankings of library services they would spend money on. A total of 65 percent felt this was 'very important'; almost identical numbers, 62 percent, though this should be a library priority. . . . Clearly, the American public agrees wholeheartedly with the library leaders that the American public library building is an intrinsic part of the library's identity. It is important to note that support for this function comes only after purchasing new books and computers and computer access, and that all three categories polled extremely well among all groups [surveyed]" (p. 26).

Crosbie, Michael J., and Damon D. Hickey. 2001. *When Change Is Set in Stone: An Analysis of Seven Academic Libraries Designed by Perry Dean Rogers & Partners: Architects.* **Chicago: American Library Association.**

Crosbie is an architectural critic who has followed the work of Perry Dean Rogers for some years. Hickey is the head librarian at The College of Wooster, where he worked with Perry Dean Rogers on two major projects. The libraries reviewed in this book are the Wyndham Robertson Library, Hollis University; the Health Sciences and Human Services Library, University of Maryland-Baltimore (UMB); the Flo K. Gault Library for Independent Study, The College of Wooster; the Waidner Library, Dickson College; the Morgan Library, Colorado State University; the Timken Science Library, The College of Wooster; and the John Deaver Drinko Library, Marshall University. The Health Sciences Library at UMB and the Drinko Library are reviewed especially favorably, though all seven libraries are praised.

Crosbie and Hickey comment from somewhat different perspectives on each of the seven libraries, identifying what is particularly successful about each building and giving some account of the design choices made by the architects. Except for the account of the Drinko Library, they give almost no attention to any academically driven planning that shaped the conception of these buildings.

Hickey writes a useful section (pp. 8-18) identifying nine factors that powerfully influenced the libraries reviewed in this book. See also Foote, below.

Demas, Sam, and Jeffrey A. Scherer. 2002. Esprit de Place: Maintaining and Designing Library Buildings to Provide Transcendent Spaces. *American Libraries* **33 (April): 65-68.**

The authors describe how libraries, both public and academic, are now being designed to respond to the wish that they be community spaces and affirm community values.

Dowler, L., ed. 1997. *Gateways to Knowledge: The Role of Academic Libraries in Teaching, Learning, and Research.* **Cambridge, Mass.: MIT Press.**

The essays of this book emphasize teaching and research more than learning. Two essays are particularly good. One is by Richard A. Lanham, "A Computer-Based Harvard Red Book: General Education in the Digital Age" (pp. 151-168). This essay takes the form of an imaginary memo from a university president to a faculty committee, charging it with reconceiving general education in the digital age, just as Harvard's President Conant appointed a committee in 1943 to ponder the objectives of a general education in a free society. The essay asks what kind of literacy students will need; considers what happens to the textbook and the classroom and what becomes of the academic major; and argues for the possibility of a central role for libraries in digitally based education. Lanham thinks with insight and writes with wit.

The other essay, entitled "Postscript" (pp. 215-228), is by Dowler. Drawing on the other essays in this volume, Dowler argues that "teaching is the core of the gateway library" (p. 219) and focuses on how students learn. "The challenge for libraries, then, is to respond to these changes in teaching and learning and create an environment for problem solving and student-centered learning" (p. 221).

James Wilkinson, in "Homesteading on the Electronic Frontier: Technology, Libraries, and Learning" (pp. 181-196), argues that "as library functions broaden with the growth of technology, librarians are expanding their own role within colleges and universities and asserting the need and desirability to act as teachers as well as custodians of information. . . . The concept of the 'librarian as teacher' acknowledges that a great deal of learning occurs in libraries (as well as in the classroom) as a result of these student research activities and that libraries are in a position to facilitate that learning. The emerging importance of technology within the library precincts also leads to the need for experts who can initiate library users into the *arcane imperii* of digital software. Just as teaching hospitals are attached to university medical schools, we can establish teaching libraries where students learn about research firsthand. . . . . But there is more. Librarians have sought to engage themselves more actively in teaching at the very time that teaching and learning themselves are being reexamined and redefined within the university as a whole. . . . In the old model, teachers actively dispensed knowledge and students passively benefited from their wisdom, but the new model increasingly emphasizes partnership, problem solving, and active learning. . . . Librarians themselves now aspire to expand their traditional reference functions to include an active partnership in teaching. And teaching itself, which both libraries and technology attempt to serve, is being reconceived as a complex process of learner-centered teaching and active learning that is guided by a teacher who is no longer a distant authority but a concerned and committed guide" (pp. 182-184). Wilkinson then asks, "Does all this mean that the library as a physical space has become obsolete? I would argue that, on the contrary, its usefulness as a teaching space remains unimpaired and may even increase. A great deal of teaching still requires direct contact to be truly effective. In general, students continue to express a wish for more interaction with faculty and with one another and not less. Just as some of the research formerly done in libraries is now done in faculty offices or student dorm rooms—with a personal computer serving as a study carrel—so can some of the group learning that formerly occurred exclusively in classrooms now take place in libraries. . . . Here it seems to me that libraries could usefully supplement or even take the lead in providing a learning environment where information technology is made available with some thought to how learning really occurs" (pp. 193-194).

Foote, Steven M. 1995. An Architect's Perspective on Contemporary Academic Library Design. *Bulletin of the Medical Library Association* **83: 351-356.**

Foote, who is president of Perry Dean Rogers, comments on the effort among library designers to find "the symbolic meaning of technology" and on the drag of traditional thinking in that effort (p. 351). See also Crosbie and Hickey, above.

Hardesty, Larry. 1995. Faculty Culture and Bibliographic Instruction: An Exploratory Essay. *Library Trends* **44: 339-367.**

Hardesty notes that academic institutions invest substantially in their libraries, which, however, are significantly underutilized by students. He further notes that most faculty members will confirm the importance of effective use of the library, but few are willing to devote class time to teaching library skills to students. Hardesty explains these apparent contradictions in terms of a pervasive culture among faculty that does not value librarians as teachers and undervalues the teaching of library skills compared to substantive disciplinary knowledge.

Hartman, Craig, John Parman, and Cheryl Paker. 1996. The Architect's Point of View. In *The National Electronic Library: A Guide to the Future for Library Managers,* **edited by Gary M. Pitkin. Wesport, Conn.: Greenwood Press.**

The authors are architects in the San Francisco office of Skidmore, Owings, & Merrill. They argue for the community functions of libraries, noting for instance that at a national accounting firm heavily invested in telecommuting, "the library had become the one remaining place where people could meet informally to share their experience and gain a sense of each other as colleagues" (p. 105). They affirm "the electronic revolution only makes human encounter, which is the real basis of community, more valuable and necessary—not less so. As communities that we now take for granted, like the workplace, lose their status as a given in our society, others—the library among them—will grow in importance" (p. 122).

Hawkins, Brian L., and Patricia Battin. 1998. *The Mirage of Continuity. Reconfiguring Academic Information Resources for the 21st Century*. Washington, D.C.: Council on Library and Information Resources and the Association of American Universities.

This highly regarded book argues the case for interpolative change in library planning. It is not particularly concerned with library space.

Heaton, Shelley, and Kenneth E. Marks. 2000. Planning the UNLV Lied Library. *Library Hi Tech* 20: 12-20.

Heaton and Marks provide a case study of a new library building, giving much attention to the intricacies of planning for a publicly financed library but little account of the academic (as distinguished from the service) objectives of the Lied Library. This issue of *Library Hi Tech* is entirely devoted to various aspects of the planning and construction of the Lied Library at the University of Nevada at Las Vegas.

Holmes-Wong, Deborah, Marianne Afifi, and Shahla Bahavar. 1997. If You Build It, They Will Come: Spaces, Values, and Services in the Digital Era. *Library Administration & Management* 11: 74-85.

This is an excellent account of the planning and success with readers of the pioneering Thomas and Dorothy Leavey Library at the University of Southern California. See also the article by Victoria Steele noted in the entry for Sue Taylor, ed., *Building Libraries for the Information Age*.

Huang, Jeffrey. 2001. Future Space: A New Blueprint for Business Architecture. *Harvard Business Review* (April): 149-158.

Huang regards teaching and learning spaces as a species of "business architecture." He reports on the effort at the Harvard Graduate School of Design and the Center for Design Informatics to develop guidelines for architectural design that bring physical and virtual space strongly together. "Although we have been designing buildings for thousands of years and Web spaces for about a decade, we have almost no experience merging the two" (p. 150).

Jones, William G. 1999. *Library Buildings: Renovation and Reconfiguration.* **SPEC Kit 244. Washington, D.C.: Association of Research Libraries.**

Jones includes reports about renovation projects at Emory, Kansas State, Yale, Columbia, and West Virginia Universities, and from the University of Washington and the University of Chicago, along with short commentaries from the architects Aaron Cohen and Geoffrey Freeman. Tellingly, Jones's checklist for project preparedness assumes that the rationale for construction is clear and compelling; the checklist asks only about community support for the project.

Library Builders. **1997. London: Academy Editions.**

This is a coffee-table book, much concerned with library buildings as sculptural attempts to capture the "idea" of libraries in general or of a particular library project. While there are a number of projects from the United States represented in the book, most are European projects.

Michael Brawne asserts in his introduction that "two primary functions occur in libraries: the storage of the information source—books, journals, maps, recorded music, CD-ROMs, and so on—and the opportunity of having access to that information by individuals at a time of their choosing. That this is a matter of a direct and individual relationship is crucial, and of primary design significance. . . . The library—and the museum—allows for individuals to decide when they need access and equally to determine what information they want" (p. 6). "We should perhaps also remember that we are social animals. Although the book or the computer provides us as individuals with information, that search may still at times be a social act. We may want to be where the pursuit of knowledge is celebrated" (p. 9).

In a chapter entitled "Interiors in Detail" (pp. 216-219), Brawne argues that "it would seem that it is difficult to establish a typology of libraries at the level of the plan and section of the whole building. What makes a building a library is a set of medium- to small-scale decisions which principally involve furniture" (p. 216).

Library Buildings Consultant List 1999. **1999. Compiled by Jonathan LeBreton for the Library Administration and Management Association. Chicago: American Library Association.**

This biennial compilation includes a bibliography (pp. viii-xi) about library design and the use of consultants.

Consultants are invited to identify the types of service (e.g., "feasibility studies," "space planning") they provide by checking against a list of 25 possible services (p. 96). The list focuses on a set of "how-to" issues and does not include items regarding the identification of problems that might prompt a project or assistance in thinking about the mission of a library and how that mission might be expressed architecturally.

Leighton, Philip D., and David C. Weber. 1999. *Planning Academic and Research Library Buildings*. 3rd ed.; 1st ed. by Keyes D. Metcalf. Chicago: American Library Association.

Leighton and Weber provide the one essential guide to planning academic libraries. See the introduction of this report for a further account of this book.

Light, Richard J. 2001. *Making the Most of College: Students Speak Their Minds*. Cambridge, Mass.: Harvard University Press.

Light investigates how and with whom students learn, but not where they learn. One might argue that the built environment for learning must be carefully considered in the effort to help students make the most of college.

Matier, Michael, and C. Clinton Sidle. 1993. What Size Libraries for 2010? *Planning for Higher Education* 21 (Summer): 9-15.

Matier and Sidle approach library planning as an exercise in housing readers and books and conclude that the outlook for digital information is so uncertain as to make changes in conventional space allocation formulas imprudent.

McCarthy, Richard C. 1999. *Designing Better Libraries: Selecting & Working with Building Professionals*. 2nd ed. Fort Atkinson, Wisc.: Highsmith Press.

This is a typical "how-to," rather than a "what-to," book.

Michaels, David L. 1994. Charette: Design in a Nutshell. *Library Administration & Management* 8: 135-138.

Michaels describes the charette as an intensely collaborative and highly productive method of architectural design.

Rettig, James R. 1998. Designing Scenarios to Design Effective Buildings. In *Recreating the Academic Library: Breaking Virtual Ground*, edited by Cheryl LaGuardia. New York: Neal-Schuman.

Rettig urges that less emphasis be given to housing collections and more to accommodating reader behaviors. "Because the ways in which the members of a university community seek, identify, and use information change with increasing rapidity and because the traditional processes for planning academic library buildings have proved inadequate for incorporating long-term flexibility, the premises and processes of building planning need to be rethought" (p. 88). This article views library users primarily as people who manipulate information, not as learners.

Schneekloth, Lynda H., and Ellen Bruce Keable. 1991. Evaluation of Library Facilities: A Tool for Managing Change. *Occasional Papers*, no. 191 (November). University of Illinois Graduate School of Library and Information Science.

Schneekloth and Keable describe postoccupancy evaluation as a tool used at the Carol M. Newman Library of Virginia Polytechnic

Institute and State University and at an unnamed special library serving a financial company.

Stage, Frances K., Patricia A. Muller, Jillian Kinzie, and Ada Simmons. 1998. *Creating Learning-Centered Classrooms: What Does Learning Theory Have to Say?* **ASHE-ERIC Higher Education Report, 26(4). Washington, D.C.: Graduate School of Education and Human Development, George Washington University.**

The authors survey six learning theories and their application to higher education teaching and learning. A table (p. 75) indicates the authors' belief that only three of these theories (attribution, self-efficacy, and learning styles) are backed with extensive research to verify or validate the theory. For the most part, there is only moderate or limited research on the application of these theories to college students, the modification of teaching methods, or the effects of the application of such theories to teaching.

Stein, Karen D. 1998. Project Diary: Henry Myerberg's First Building as a Solo Architect, the Rhys Carpenter Library, Provides Bryn Mawr College with a Popular New Campus Center. *Architectural Record* **186 (February): 82-91.**

Stein's article serves as a reminder and a good case study of the stop-and-start character of many library projects and of the way project scope, design, technical challenges, and cost can change over the long periods of time normally required to bring projects to completion.

Sutton, Lynn Sorensen. 2000. Imagining Learning Spaces at Wayne State University's New David Adamany Undergraduate Library. *Research Strategies* **17: 139-146.**

Sutton describes the Adamany Library as "intentionally not designed to be collection-intensive" (p. 140), but to be "dedicated solely to student success" (p. 139).

Taylor Sue, ed. 1995. *Building Libraries for the Information Age.* **Based on the proceedings of a Symposium on the Future of Higher Education Libraries, King's Manor, York, April 11–12, 1994. York: Institute of Advanced Architectural Studies, University of York.**

The symposium was prompted by the Follett report on the future of academic libraries in the United Kingdom. The Higher Education Funding Councils Libraries Review Group was charged in 1992 and reported in December 1993. Sir Brian Follett chaired the review group.

In effect, the Follett report constituted a nationwide academic planning effort for libraries, tied to the fiscal responsibilities of the then-new Higher Education funding Councils.

According to Lynne J. Brindley's introduction to the volume (pp. 1-4), the Follett report was written in response to "the mass expansion of student numbers" and the perceived failure of libraries "in their fundamental task of providing enough books and enough seats for students" (p. 1).

The report "endorsed the view that there needs to be what it calls a sea-change in the way institutions plan and provide for the information needs of those working within them. The traditional view of the library as the single repository of the information needed for teaching, learning and research is woefully inadequate. . . . Follett endorsed the move from holdings to access, and called on universities to take a strategic view of information provision, and for information and its management to be fully integrated with academic and institutional planning.

"On support for teaching and learning, on how to make it better for the students, the Report offers no panaceas. Most importantly in this context, a major, funded space initiative was proposed to build, remodel and adapt space for library use, with a particular focus on service delivery and innovation using technology, rather than simply providing more space to accumulate materials. . . .

"On the research side the strategy argued for was one of national and regional collaboration, involving specialisation and cooperation. . . .

"The Information Technology group focused particularly on how developments in IT might be harnessed to underpin change across the whole academic library sector" (pp. 1-2).

This book publishes brief papers given at the symposium, including a few general commentaries and several case studies of new library buildings. The papers include Victoria Steele, "Producing Value: A North American Perspective on the Future of Higher Education Libraries" (pp. 77-80), commenting on the Thomas and Dorothy Leavey Library at the University of Southern California.

Andrew McDonald provides an account of some of the building activity that followed the Follett report in "Planning Academic Library Buildings for a New Age: Some Principles, Trends, and Developments in the United Kingdom," *Advances in Librarianship* 24 (2000), 51-79.

Van Slyck, Abigail A. 2000. Libraries: A New Chapter. *Architectural Record* 188 (October): 151-153.

Writing in the "Building Types Study 790," on academic and public libraries, Van Slyck observes that "the return of the monumental reading room is part of the growing acknowledgement that the library is as much about social interaction and intellectual exchange as the storage of books and the delivery of discrete packages of information into the hands of an individual reader." She notes there is nothing new in this idea, as libraries built in the nineteenth-century and earlier often affirmed quite strongly the social character of knowledge.

Webb, T. D., ed. 2000. *Building Libraries for the 21st Century: The Shape of Information*. Jefferson, N.C.: McFarland.

Webb collects a set of essays mostly about individual new library buildings—national, academic, and public. The following are notable among these essays:

Charlene Hurt, "The Johnson Center Library at George Mason University" (pp. 83-104) presents a model case study, giving ample attention to what motivated the new library and placing it strongly in campus-wide thinking about space for learning. In a separate article, "Building Libraries in the Virtual Age," published in 1997 (*College & Research Libraries News* 58 [February]: 75-76, 91), Hurt observes that "experiential learning takes place anywhere, any time, in a variety of environments, often social. . . . The popularity of bookstores that serve drinks and food demonstrates a preference for a more casual, social environment [in libraries], as does our students' preference for seating in highly visible areas" (pp. 75-76).

John Ober's essay, Library Services at California State University, Monterey Bay (pp. 122-127), is an interesting case study of an entire institution created at the former Fort Ord in less than two years. Ober reports that all planning, including that for the library, was strongly influenced by the mission statement of the new Monterey Bay campus, which is reproduced in this article. Most interestingly, California State University, Monterey Bay (CSUMB) Chancellor Barry Munitz felt the new campus did not require a traditional library. Dr. James May was appointed dean of Science, Technology and Information Resources and "he spent much of his energy convincing administrators, including Chancellor Munitz, that a physical library with a collection of print materials was necessary at CSUMB; the appropriate use of technology to provide access to undergraduate level resources could and should be a cornerstone of library services but would not be sufficient in and of itself" (p. 126). Ober describes the wide press coverage that the ensuing debate about the library received, and its outcome in the decision to build a library with a relatively small core collection of print materials.

Another interesting essay is "The Academic Library in the 21st Century: Partner in Education," by Geoffrey T. Freeman, (pp. 168-175). Written by an architect, the essay argues ably for the educational function of libraries.

Wiley, Peter Booth. 1997. Beyond the Blueprint. *Library Journal,* **122 (Feb. 15): 110-113.**

Wiley describes several kinds of postoccupancy adjustments made in large city public libraries as a result of experience with the buildings after they were open.